A Dark Journey

A Dark Journey

Anna S. Cornell

ISBN-13: 9780692544556
ISBN-10: 0692544550

Dedication

This book is dedicated to my daughter, Lauren, who gives me life.

Lauren:*

I never wanted to break up our family and have you alternating between two different houses. I divorced your father to protect you and so you wouldn't grow up thinking it was acceptable for a man to treat a woman the way your father treated me. I love you with all that is in me, and I will give my heart and soul to raise you to be a good and successful woman. Just remember that life is unfair at times, and not all decisions are easy ones. Mommy suffered and still suffers so that you won't have to. I live and breathe for you. I promise I will never give up on you, and I want only your well-being. You always tell me we're a team. Like a team, we can do great things for ourselves and others. While many may tell you otherwise, just remember
that I adore you.

---

* Name has been changed to protect both privacy and identity.

MY FIRST TWENTY-SIX YEARS

Where do we learn the nature of love? I learned it in my parents' home in a small, rural town in Lebanon. My parents are devout Lebanese Catholics who live the life of their faith. From the beginning of our lives, they showered my four sisters and me with a very special kind of love—a mixture of kindness, discipline, laughter, and compassion. I never heard my parents argue and never saw any dissension between them. They were devoted to their children, but above all, they were devoted to one another. The children's wishes did not come before their own, but this did not create any conflict. Always kind, generous, and gracious to family, friends, and neighbors, they taught us to be the same—welcoming and accepting.

My parents graciously hosted friends, family, and relatives. It's difficult to imagine any type of food not offered at our table or any request for help refused. My dad not only treated us five daughters like princesses, but he also spoiled my mom like she was one of us. I remember how she would wake up with him very early in the morning and prepare his coffee, and they would discuss their plans for the day. Then, she would wait for him to come home to have lunch or dinner with him, and they shared every detail of what had happened since they had parted—whatever they had said or heard. They were, and still are, best friends. They lifted each other up. They praised each other. If my dad got sick, then my mom got sicker; if my mom was unhappy, then my dad became very sad. He would call her from work to check on her and hear her voice, and she would always treat him like a king.

My mom looked at my dad as the best gentleman who ever existed, and my dad honored my mom's wishes and needs. He was always generous with his in-laws and acted like a son to her father and mother. My parents never disagreed in front of their children, and they always had a common goal. My dad was the man of the house, and he acted like one. But he also knew and acknowledged that his success was due in part to the way my mom managed the house and raised us. My childhood was healthy, and it was fun. It was sad sometimes, but we all gathered every night for snacks and discussion. We always went to church together on Sunday and visited many people afterward as part of the fun social culture in Lebanon.

With my vision of love and marriage so deeply rooted in my own wonderful parents, I set out to make my life and find a man with whom I could share this way of loving. I wanted the same cocktail of love and friendship mixed with trust and overwhelming compassion that was my parents' marriage. I hoped I would find it in my travels, which began in my late teenage years.

Being the oldest of five daughters definitely came with lots of responsibilities and accountability, but being the oldest had its own special privileges too. I was pampered and dolled up all the time yet very disciplined. I grew up getting what I wanted, yet knowing how hard it must have been for my parents to provide without a single complaint. I was always observant and considerate of my family. I worried about my parents all the time and still do. Their wellbeing never left my thoughts, and I did all I could to help my sisters advance in life. I was always given choices, but I had to learn to take responsibility for my actions. Because of all this, I grew up to be very independent.

My mother was an exceptional role model for us. She dedicated every day to preparing meals and cleaning and keeping the house in order. Every afternoon after we came home from school, she fed us, helped us with our homework, and listened to our concerns. This was a time when she shared herself and her values with us. Home felt safe; home felt normal. My parents knew when to let go and when to give in. They helped me manage my priorities in life as I grew up, and they relentlessly encouraged me to be the best I could be. At the same time, they taught me to stay humble, helpful, generous, and mindful of others and the environment. Indeed, their lessons, which I never thought resonated with me in my teens, made a huge difference in how I now lead my life every day.

Even though I was accepted to dentistry school in Lebanon, I preferred to venture into genetic engineering and make a difference in people's longevity. I had lost a dear aunt to kidney disease; she died of the disease before her name came up on the waiting list for a kidney transplant. I decided to pursue my studies abroad like many Lebanese students. I travelled to the United States of America at the age of eighteen, where I lived with an uncle who graciously took me in. I spent my first couple of years in the United States attending a community college. The first two years were challenging on all fronts. Because I spoke only Lebanese and French, I could only study and understand the material explained in class by translating every word in my textbooks. The dictionary was my constant companion and best friend. Even so, I often used the wrong word in conversation. Although I faced many culture shocks; none stopped me from pursuing my goal. At the community college, I finished my double associate's degree in chemistry and physics before I transferred with a full scholarship to Cornell University to pursue bachelor's and master's degrees in biological and environmental engineering.

Throughout college, I worked many kinds of jobs to help me pay for expenses. I had to pay tuition at the community college and during my graduate studies. Then, there were books to purchase, living expenses, and any extracurricular activities I needed to participate in. I worked in a coffee shop and as a veterinary technician, tutored private science lessons, taught graduate courses at the university, helped as a receptionist in the university hotel, and much more. My goal was always to do my best and succeed no matter how menial the job might have been. I took all the work very seriously, yet I had fun doing each job. I believe I performed every task with dignity.

All during college and graduate school, I had a wonderful circle of friends who depended on me and always wanted to have me around. They looked on me as trustworthy and reliable and enjoyed my liveliness and positive energy. My apartment was often full of my friends for whom I prepared meals and helped with schoolwork and job applications. I was very pleased that my apartment was considered a warm, friendly place.

I faced only one major setback during those years. In the last few months of my senior year at Cornell, my doctor discovered that I had a tumor behind my lungs. I underwent two biopsies, and my doctor determined that it was necessary for me to have surgery as quickly as possible. Fortunately, the results of the surgery were negative for cancer; I was not dying as I had feared, and I had many more than four months to live. Rather, I had a whole lifetime ahead of me—many, many days in which to love and cherish every bonus minute I was given.

These events dramatically changed my perspective on life. They made me stronger and happier and much less tolerant of negativity and what I saw as unnecessary evil. I resumed my studies and graduated from Cornell with honors. After completing my master's degree and an intensive thesis, I moved to California to start work in the information technology world. It was a blessed move, yet I had no idea what IT was, and I took it upon myself to study night and day for six weeks before I took off for my first project in Naperville, Illinois. I continued working hard while fighting to stay in the United States and finding the right company to sponsor my work visa, which I did. The road to my success was a smooth one. I moved up from an entry-level analyst to senior analyst, from senior analyst to project manager, and then from project manager to product manager in less than four years. It was a whirlwind rise in a fascinating world that probably would have continued, but seven and a half years after leaving Lebanon, the focus of my world changed.

With my privileged and blessed upbringing and so many fine opportunities, it's no wonder that I was a happy, outgoing person and a very trusting one. My parents, relatives, and friends accepted me. I never felt that any expectations my parents had were unreasonable. I was successful academically, professionally, and socially, with a wide circle of friends. My family, friends, and I believed in each other; we didn't ask each other to prove ourselves or justify our thoughts and actions. I never felt negatively challenged; I certainly wasn't criticized for the clothes I wore, my choices in food, my preferences in beverages, or the way I kept my apartment. I felt free to be myself. All that would change when I selected the man I believed would be my life's partner.

Searching for Love

After achieving so many of my dreams, I began to open up to the possibility of love in a long-term commitment. I created an account with an online dating service. My future husband, Jason,* contacted me on that account in early 2010, and we agreed to have a phone conversation. It was marvelous; we talked for seven hours, and I felt that I wanted very much to get to know this man. Jason was of Lebanese descent on his father's side and Palestinian on his mother's side, He had received his medical degree in Jordan. Because he wanted to practice medicine in the United States, he was living in New Jersey and completing a three-year residency. We met in the middle of his second year of residency. We had many long, sweet, laughter-filled conversations that made us both want to meet face-to-face. I'm sure I was in love with him after our first conversation.

We made our plans, and I flew to New Jersey one month later. We were together for a long weekend. He was a perfect gentleman—walking me to my hotel room door, showing great manners. We walked in the parks, stopped for coffee, and just talked and talked. Jason was so busy with his residency that we had to make every minute together count. To me, Jason appeared independent and cosmopolitan. More importantly, he spoke of good values—family values. He said I would be his new family. We would be a good Christian family, loving and encouraging one another.

---

*Name has been changed to protect both privacy and identity.

We took the Staten Island Ferry. Like a gentleman, he took off his jacket and put it on me since it was chilly and windy. We got to New York, and we held hands and ran in the streets like two lovebirds. It felt wonderfully surreal, and I felt safe with Jason. We took lots of pictures and had dinner at an Indonesian restaurant. It was a new and fun experience for me.

When we got back to the car at the end of our New York day trip, we had our first kiss—tentative at first, but then passionate. Jason claimed he had never kissed a girl before or slept with one. That seemed strange to me, but I believed him; I had no reason not to. After four years of marriage and more lies than I can count, however, I wonder now about most things Jason told me.

I went back to California feeling wonderful. Jason was a handsome man, tall and dark. He was intelligent, kind, and well mannered, and he made me feel very special. Up to that time, I had not been what you'd call "lucky in love." There had never been a mutual spark between me and any other man. Sometimes I would be very attracted to a man who didn't feel the same for me; sometimes it was the other way around. But now I felt I had met a man who felt the same way about me as I felt about him. He was the man with whom I'd be able to have a full, loving relationship. Jason was the one; we were made for each other.

STRANGENESS

We visited each other three more times before Jason and I got married in September 2010, only six months after we met. Five months before our marriage, we met in Las Vegas, where we roamed around like two little kids, taking pictures everywhere and having late night dinners. He didn't directly complain about money or expenses then, although he didn't like us paying money to see the aquarium in Mandalay Bay. He also was hesitant to buy coffee every time I bought mine, and he didn't offer to pay for it. I was independent, so I didn't hold it against him even though this behavior seemed very odd and inconsistent with the way other men had treated me. Then he bought us tickets to see *Le Cirque de Soleil* in the Wynn Hotel. At the end of the show, he caught a rose that was thrown by the artist and gave it to me, and I thought that was heroic and romantic. I kept and treasured that rose for a very long time.

The inconsistency between his frugality and generosity didn't strike me at the time. It would later, though, when he became more and more controlling of my spending. Gradually, Jason began to tell me what I could buy and what I couldn't. It wasn't so much that he cared, I think, but that he wanted power over me. I never knew what he really wanted because on one day he'd tell me not to buy bottled water, and on the next it was OK if I did. Keeping me guessing was one way he manipulated and controlled me. At this point, the things Jason was trying to control were minor and only mildly irritating.

This pattern did not fully develop or expand to more important things until after our marriage.

But our visit to Las Vegas was overshadowed by something else—something truly strange and unsettling. We had talked of marriage, and we were pretty much determined that we would marry. We went to a hotel room, and Jason asked me if I was a virgin. He said he wouldn't marry me if I had been with another man. Of course I was a virgin! But he insisted on "examining" me, even though he is not a gynecologist. Only after this examination and interrogation did we make love.

My first sexual experience was far from what I had dreamed it would be; it seemed part of the clinical examination. This crazy insistence on "proof" disturbed me, but I knew myself—I knew I was a virgin—and I believed I really wanted to marry Jason. I accepted this first instance of humiliation and just kept believing in our love for each other. Had I told my family about this occurrence, they would surely have advised me to run for my life. I was simply too embarrassed to tell anyone of Jason's treatment of me. To my dismay, Jason's attempts to humiliate me only increased as our relationship progressed.

Four months after our first contact, Jason came to San Francisco, and he stayed at my apartment. During his visit, I heard Jason talking to his sister on the phone. She wasn't happy about his staying with me since his family believed him to be a virgin and respectful to a woman until the wedding day. Jason said he didn't want to spend money on a hotel, and that's what he kept explaining to her over the phone. This conversation lasted a long time, with Jason desperately trying to justify himself to his sister. This was my first exposure to the influence Jason's family had over him.

Even though he continued to stay with me during that trip, I felt the intrusion of his family into our lives. I couldn't understand then why Jason would tell his family anything about our intimacy. As the years went by, I learned that he kept no part of our life together private from them. When it suited him, he would tell half-truths and even misrepresent things so that he looked good to them and I looked like the villain. As I slowly began to learn in very sad and harsh ways, Jason's relationship with his family was much closer than his relationship with me.

I tried to talk to Jason's sister on the phone several times. At first, she was simply very cold, but she grew less distant as time went on. Unfortunately, we never did form a good or trustful relationship. She always seemed to be suspicious of me. Later, when I met Jason's parents, I was able to understand her distance. They are crazily protective and controlling of one another and seem to see anyone outside the family as the enemy. This feeling extends even to members of the extended family. Jason told me that his mother competes with her sisters and is proud that her children are smarter and better behaved than her nieces and nephews. It is such a contrast to my wonderful family; their way of life is almost alien to me—as mine must be to them.

Even so, Jason and I enjoyed some of our time together in California. I took him around to every possible happy place I had been to. We traveled around the northern part of the state, and I showed him beautiful places— Camel, Monterey, Half Moon Bay, San Francisco, the Golden Gate Bridge, the San Mateo Bridge. But it was during this visit that Jason began displaying another disturbing characteristic. I know it now as jealousy, but it appeared to me then as insecurity. We met some of my Lebanese friends in downtown San Jose, CA, and Jason was cold and didn't try to enter the conversation. I frantically overcompensated for his silence that seemed like disdain. It was embarrassing for my friends and me, and from then on, I dreaded the minute I would have to introduce him to anyone else. It seemed that he always felt insecure and uncomfortable around my friends. My friends must have been hurt by Jason's actions, but they never said anything to me about their feelings. Nor did they criticize him to me. I know now that they just didn't want to hurt me.

He also was sickeningly judgmental. When we were alone again, he would make comments about each of them and about even the slightest detail. To Jason, my friends were "low class." He thought their conversations were "superficial and useless." He imagined characteristics that weren't there and would make up things about them and try to convince me to believe what he said. Jason couldn't handle being with people who were very educated—people like my friends who understood business and technology and investing. He always had to be the one who knew it all.

When he didn't, the only way he could maintain his self-esteem was by putting other people down.

As hard as I tried to defend my friends, Jason would not change his mind about them. He continued to call them "low class" and "superficial." He insisted angrily that they were not good enough for me; it was not appropriate for me to be with them. Then he would try to create guilt in me by arguing that he was my life now, and I should not even need friends, especially those "beneath" me (and him, I'm sure). Jason was so positive in telling me these things that I began to question myself and to believe him. I stopped seeing these friends, hoping that if I did so Jason would love me more. However, he used this type of manipulation over and over in our life together, and I lost more and more friends. Sadly, Jason's love for me did not increase.

The whole event was so unsettling, it made me wonder if I should share with him or tell him anything because it seemed to be getting me in trouble. When he didn't approve of something I said or did, he would start in with his usual yelling. He would insist that I was not committed to him and had become too Americanized. Then he would get a very sorrowful look on his face and tell me all he wanted was a "good, conservative Arabic woman."

Small things about me seemed to bother him. He had seen my lifestyle and observed many small details. For instance, I only drank bottled water, and I always had a pack of it in the trunk of my car. I often went to the drive-through at Starbucks. I regularly had manicures and pedicures, and I shopped when I needed to. Jason was well aware of my behaviors and made negative comments about them. But that didn't seem significant at the time because he didn't have any say over them, and I couldn't imagine that he ever would. His criticism about these very small things increased over the months of our engagement, but I felt no real discomfort about that. Such little disagreements would certainly iron themselves out, I believed. How could I have imagined how many more of them would arise as we set up housekeeping together?

ENGAGEMENT

The day of our actual engagement was more bitter than sweet. It happened six months after we met and two months after our stay in San Francisco. First, Jason's father asked my father for my hand *over the phone*. Having this conversation from a distance is most untypical in the Lebanese culture. Our families only lived four hours apart, but my parents and I accepted it. My family wanted to make it possible for me to do what made me happy, and I was satisfied that the customary request had been made.

Jason and I had talked by phone about how we would get engaged. We agreed that I would come to New Jersey for the weekend, and Jason arranged to have the time off from his residency to do what we wanted on that weekend. I had even arranged to have a priest bless the rings. I knew Jason was going to give me the engagement ring in Central Park. In my excitement and pride, I asked a friend to take a quick lunch break from his hectic banking day and meet us nearby. I was proud of Jason and wanted my friend to meet him; I wanted to show him off. But Jason's insecurity resulted in absurd behavior. He shouted loud, long insults and made threatening gestures toward me as my friend was approaching and continued doing so after we met him. Although all the insults were directed at me, my friend became very upset. All that ugly display because my friend was a man.

Jason stormed off, and I had to run after him in Central Park like an idiot and beg him to calm down, but he didn't. At one point, he even said he didn't want to marry me. Astonished and deeply hurt, I said it was OK not to marry me, but

I begged him to stop embarrassing me. Thankfully, he calmed down a bit. We walked to the Boat House in Central Park, where his demeanor changed dramatically. It was as if the curtain had come down between acts of a play. Jason turned to me, took off his outer shirt, and revealed a T-shirt printed with our picture and the "Will You Marry Me!" He was immediately sweet and loving as though nothing angry has passed between us. I was so much in love with him that I simply embraced the happiness he offered, never dreaming that his actions indicated the kind of manipulation that would keep me in his power for several years.

I felt bad that I had gotten him so upset. Jason presented me with a short poem and formally proposed to me. In spite of his strange—even cruel—behavior, I couldn't say no. I forgave him. It's hard now to understand why I did. I know I felt bad because I had interrupted his plan by asking my friend to join us. I saw that Jason was angry mostly because he had planned what he thought was a dramatic, romantic moment, and I had messed it up. He had prepared the moment carefully—the act of the engagement seemed to mean so much to him. Even though he was angry, he wouldn't waste his plans. To make his dream of a magical engagement scene come true, he had to take away his threat to call the wedding off. Later on, I found out that Jason had shared the poem with his family and extended family beforehand to get their approval and compliments. No matter what, he had to make himself look good in their eyes.

I know I'm a people-pleaser, and I always want to believe in the good of people. I just believed things would get better—they had to! I can see now that overlooking Jason's behavior and blaming myself were the beginning to a most unhealthy relationship. I began to convince myself that I was wrong, that I was the cause of Jason's outbursts. And I began to change from the independent, trusting woman I had been into a woman who would change her behavior in order to avoid her husband's anger. But it was years before I understood this, and that day we proceeded to plan our wedding to be held near my home town in Lebanon six months after our first meeting.

That same night, we went to the home of my uncle and aunt in New Jersey to receive a Christian blessing on our engagement. A priest came and blessed us. We had a lovely dinner with no tension, and the crazy engagement day ended happily—or so it seemed.

Early Signs

During this time before our marriage, there were some signs of cruelty and weirdness on Jason's part, but I chose to ignore them. For example, he often judged me harshly just for being myself and belittled me because I had university loans—that I paid off by myself to the last dollar—and because my family was not rich. He constantly told me, "Manni majbour itjawwaz mara madyouneh." ("I don't have to marry a woman with loans and debt."). He would add, "I should marry a rich girl." Yes, Jason's parents had more money and a bigger house than my parents, but their living standard was not really above ours. They worked hard to acquire money, yet it seemed their whole purpose was to have it and to belittle those who had less and lived in smaller houses. They hated loans and looked down on my parents for not ensuring that I would not have to take out loans for my education.

I accepted all Jason's insults because I was in love with him. However, as you will see, my acquiescence only empowered him more and gave him more control to rule my world. For example, Jason, members or his family, and others communicated about the Bible and religious matters. They would send e-mails containing quotes, essays, and the like. Jason would send them on to me though I was not at all interested in them. He wanted me to respond to all the forwarded e-mails he sent me. If I didn't, he would scream and yell at me and send me mean e-mails that told me I had to answer every forwarded message. At this time, Jason's screaming made me fearful, and I'd do anything to stop it. Even though it took time from my work, I responded to all the e-mails, stupid as that seems. I just wanted to keep Jason calm. Before I met him, I had never been yelled at by anyone; I simply did not understand this kind of behavior. Again, I was sure it would stop as our love for each other grew and deepened.

As the time of our engagement passed, another of Jason's disturbing personality traits became evident: his stinginess. He would remind me of how much he paid every time he took me out to dinner or lunch. He would calculate every penny and tell me that he spent that many dollars to make me appreciate him more. I thought these actions were strange, overly frugal, and decidedly unattractive, but I was in still love with him, so I pushed my concerns over these behaviors to the side. I continued to believe things would improve between us as we got closer to our wedding day. I trusted that he would come to accept me as I had accepted him.

Another strange, unsettling thing occurred during this time. Jason insisted on seeing not only my complete medical records, but also those of my parents. I don't know exactly what he was looking for. We had already set the wedding date, but he wouldn't let up until he got what he wanted. He told me that if any kind of problems showed up, he wouldn't marry me because he didn't want his children to have health difficulties. None showed up, but Jason made me feel that he was incredibly honorable and generous in overlooking the risk caused by my father's heart disease. He didn't focus on my cancer scare because it was very clear from the records that I did not have cancer. At the time, although this behavior was cruel, I chose to see it as simply meddlesome and irritating. Once again, I did what he asked of me and hoped that would make him happy.

Not content to involve only me, Jason tried to inject himself between my friends and me. I often spent time with a certain couple. The husband was a coworker of mine, and he and I often had coffee in the cafeteria. His wife knew this and saw no problem with it since I also often did things with both of them together. We all trusted each other as friends do. After one occasion on which I had coffee with the husband, Jason had the audacity to phone my friend's wife to tell her about it. He was accusatory of both her husband and me. He thought we were both being unfaithful by just having coffee together. She was uncomfortable and very frightened. She called me to ask if everything was all right and to find out why Jason was yelling at her on the phone. All I could tell her was that it seemed Jason didn't want me to hang out with male friends even for a coffee at work. I explained that he did not believe friendship between a man and a woman was possible, and he wanted to make sure I wouldn't have any male friends. I felt embarrassed, awkward, humiliated, and I wanted to hide far away.

Even though his actions had been wrong and hurtful, Jason took no blame. He found ways to justify himself no matter what I said. He always turned things around to show that I had caused the whole problem. My words got nowhere with him, and I finally just gave up. I thought then that I was dealing with the most possessive, jealous, unloving, manipulative man I had ever met. Jason would deny that he did anything wrong no matter what had happened. He would pretend to be innocent and justify himself in a hundred ways. I would become so confused that I couldn't fight back. In that way, Jason manipulated me into accepting his wrongdoing as somehow being right. It would take me several years of accepting his self-righteous explanations of his hurtful behaviors before I could see them for what it were and learn to defend myself against them.

There were other forms of emotional abuse all during the time we dated. Jason was determined that I should see myself as less than him, so he attacked me through my family. He said my parents favored my sisters and made me come to the United States to get my education on my own without their support. (This was not true; my parents gave me both emotional and financial support.) He criticized them for making me take out student loans. He scorned their plans for our wedding, saying they were materialistic and wanted to spend too much. This was Jason trying to teach me the lesson that my family couldn't possibly love me as much as he did. Was he jealous of them? Perhaps. I always defended my family against these attacks, but Jason never gave in. Most of the time, he argued me into silence because I knew I could never change his mind. I was always very sad when he insulted my family this way and said things that were definitely not true.

He criticized my friends and didn't want me to see them. He told me I couldn't be a confidante for male friends, and I couldn't have friendships with men or even women as the next step. He played cruel games to test my love. Once, he asked, "If your father and I were in a fire, which would you save first?" Jason made me use phone cards to call my parents, but he would get ones with very few minutes, so I hardly got to speak with them. Even though we were not married at the time, he wanted complete control over my actions, and I gave into this demand. If he was there when I called them, he would make signs to tell me I'd talked long enough.

As these odd behaviors accelerated and deepened, I became more and more fearful that I didn't really know the man I had consented to marry. I became desperate to have more time to learn about him. Three months before the wedding, I tried to break off the engagement. I told him he was overbearing and insulting. His distrust and his constant questions made me angry and fearful; I needed to feel more confident in the man I was to marry.

Jason was furious, but his fury lasted only a short time. Very quickly, he called me and began to cry and say how sorry he was. I had never heard a man cry before; I was startled. I listened to him, and he sounded truly sincere. I felt sorry for him and even sorry for my doubts. Being what I see now as hopelessly naïve, I believed that when he said he was sorry, this meant that he intended to change, that he would be kind, calm, loving, and considerate. On that basis, the basis of my own naïve dreams, I agreed to continue with the engagement and wedding plans. Of course, I had doubts, but I pushed them away. After all, I believed I truly loved this man, and I had faith that he would change.

But Jason was only sorry that his plans had been endangered. I learned the hard way that he wasn't sorry for the yelling, for the demands, for the erratic behavior. More sadly, I learned that he had no intention of changing anything! Looking at myself in this, though, I have to admit that I had another misconception: I believed that I could change Jason. That I could work with the negative aspects of his character and change them to positive ones. I believed so strongly in the power of a good marriage like the one my parents had that I was sure as we lived together, shared our lives, and became ever more intimate, Jason would become better—would become everything I wanted in a husband.

Preparing for the Wedding

Jason's need to control me grew even as I was in Lebanon preparing for the wedding. I went to my parents' home in Lebanon three weeks before the wedding. One morning after I arrived, Jason called my mother in Lebanon. Like a crazy person, he yelled that I was no good: *I had smoked a cigarette!* (Someone had seen me do this in New Jersey and told Jason.) My mother didn't tell me about the call until years later; she didn't want to upset me at the time. But Jason also phoned me about the cigarette. His anger over such a small thing shocked me. When I could get a word in over his ranting, I tried to explain that I smoked only occasionally when stressed. He would hear none of it and said he was breaking off the wedding. Can you imagine? Canceling a wedding because of a cigarette? This seemed so absurd to me, but I had to deal with it. I did not want the humiliation of canceling the wedding. I did not understand how this small incident could cause so much anger in Jason. I begged, pleaded, and promised that I would never smoke again. He finally calmed down, but this behavior made my family and me very anxious. I was beginning to feel I had no freedom from Jason's prying and controlling. It seemed I couldn't avoid breaking Jason's rules—rules I would learn about only after I had violated them. But in the end, all the rules aimed at the same thing:

making me into the person Jason wanted me to be and taking away the person I really am.

Jason's stinginess also became more striking as we planned the wedding. It is the custom in our country that the groom or his family pays for the wedding. Even though his family pretended otherwise, it was clear that Jason was the one who was paying for ours. He constantly complained about the wedding expenses, and he would check everything with his family to make sure they were happy and satisfied. Even Jason's dad would not give my dad the money for the wedding expenses until after he went down to Lebanon to double- and triple-check the invoices himself.

My family didn't feel at ease. Being so generous and giving, they felt we were dealing with the wrong type of people, but they never wanted to bother me with these concerns because they thought I was happy. Years passed before my parents confided in me about their misgivings during this time. I believed whatever Jason told me about his financial situation, and I was not aware at that time of the dynamic between him and his family. He told me repeatedly, "I have nineteen thousand dollars in savings. That's all we can spend, including the honeymoon." We would start our married life living only on the income from our two jobs. My parents and I were sensitive to this financial situation and worked within this budget.

Making final decisions about the wedding felt like tug-of-war. My sisters, parents, and I would decide on a venue. I would tell Jason, and then he would tell his parents. They expressed concern over the cost, and the message from them would go through Jason to me. Because of the peculiar dynamics in Jason's family, there never could be direct communication between me or my parents and his parents. Jason was the go-between: he stated all the decisions, but they had been made by all three of them.

After what seemed like endless back and forth, we settled for the least expensive of the venues acceptable to my family and me. Lady Luck shined on us, though. Two weeks before our wedding, the reception room we had booked—the smallest in the hotel—burned out. The management upgraded us for free to the largest of the reception rooms, which was elegant and beautifully decorated. It was unfortunate for the hotel, but for my family, that was the single bright spot in all the planning.

Then there was the bickering about the menu. Again, cost was the main concern of Jason's family. The way they responded to the smallest request was humiliating. Everything was about money; there was no sense of happiness in the anticipation of what should be the most important day in their son's life. Their haggling made it seem like they felt they were giving money to a beggar. I learned later that Jason's parents told him my family was greedy and materialistic. Nonetheless, we made the very best selection possible within the small budget they allowed. Through all of this, my father preferred to let me make the choices I wanted, and he would pay the difference. But understanding that such an action would humiliate Jason's parents, he refrained. We made the very best out of what Jason's family was willing to pay for.

The wedding was to be held in a town near my home in Lebanon. Jason flew into Lebanon from New Jersey a few days before the wedding, and my dad and I picked him up at the airport. My family had prepared a welcoming feast for him, and he spent several nights before the wedding with us. Even in light of my family's graciousness, Jason kept complaining to me about my family's behavior. He said he couldn't understand why we offered him so much food and why it seemed we wasted so much instead of cooking just enough. He complained that my parents' house was small and didn't fit us all. He professed to be sorry that he had inconvenienced my sisters since they had to go sleep at my grandparents' house. But his intentions weren't good ones. He merely wanted to criticize the size and mediocrity of the house where I was born and brought up. He was very disrespectful.

Since the bride's parents pay for the prewedding reception, my dad finally felt he could do things the way he wanted. The night before the wedding, our home was overflowing with relatives and friends. Large tables with foods of all kinds were set up for the many guests who came to wish us well. I felt uplifted by the excitement and happiness shown by all of them.

They showered me with gifts and brought beautiful flowers to perfume our home. It was magical.

Many families from Jason's side in Jordan made it to Lebanon for the reception. We welcomed them like our own. I met many members of Jason's extended family, and I blended with them right away. The feeling was mutual, and it lasted through every visit I had with them. I never doubted that they loved and respected me. Jason's mother, on the other hand, was stiff and just observed the festivities most of the time rather than joining in. But when she saw her sisters taking the lead in dancing with me, she danced too. She wouldn't allow herself to be outdone by others. That night, Jason went with his family to the hotel, and I had my last single night with my family.

The Wedding

The day of the wedding started at 5:00 a.m. with hair and makeup and photography sessions. People flooded into my house to escort me to church, as is traditional. Jason's parents and siblings came over as well to take me out of my parental house, symbolically accepting me as their own. They dressed me with matching gold necklace, earrings, a ring, and a bracelet. Unfortunately, my ride was late, and his parents weren't happy about it. In fact, his mother said in a loud and angry voice, "Get out of the house; you are making my son wait" Thankfully, my family didn't hear this because my dad would not have responded pleasantly.

When my ride came, we finally left and headed to church. It was a beautiful Christian Orthodox church on the Mediterranean Sea. Jason was waiting for me outside, and his mother went to stand next to him. I was sorry for this because it is not part of the tradition. I figured out later that she just wanted to be the center of attention. My dad and his dad gave me to Jason, and the wedding ceremony began.

It's important for me to say here that Jason mislead me about his religion. I am a Catholic, but it is traditional in my country to follow the man's denomination, so the Mass was Orthodox. Although he was baptized Christian Orthodox and that's the religion stated on his passport, he does not practice that faith. His mother converted to Church of Christ, and that's the religion in which she raised her family and which is Jason's true religious affiliation.

His grandmother belongs to the Jehovah's Witnesses. When I learned this after our marriage, I was both angry and sad—angry because he had deceived me and sad because I believe it is better for married people to share a religion and raise their children in that religion.

I began to understand Jason's deception about his religion as I learned more about his parents' attitudes. I saw very little true religious faith in Jason's family. They let Jason keep secrets from me and encouraged him to break ties with me as long as he kept his strong ties with them. Jason's parents were always first to judge. They were never content but always nagging and morose. Jason grew up with all this deceit and hypocrisy; it's no wonder that he deceived me too.

After the ceremony, we headed to the hotel for the reception. The room in which the reception was held was magnificent. Greek statuary and decoration with many flowers set the mood for a most festive occasion. There were 250 guests, and everyone had a wonderful time. Music and much dancing, many toasts, and lively conversation all made this a picture-perfect wedding celebration. Jason was cooperative and pleasant throughout, but his mother made a pest of herself by repeatedly coming to stand behind him at the wedding party's table—wanting as ever to be seen as important. My sisters and I got Jason's family and guests to join in the dancing. No one heard any complaining or negative words for most of the night.

Of course, something had to go wrong, and there was one glitch. My sister had collected pictures of my childhood up through my graduation and put them on a disc. For our reception, the DJ put together a slideshow and displayed the pictures on a screen during the dinner. We had asked Jason's family to do the same several weeks earlier and give the disc to the DJ to play it also during dinner. But Jason's sister sent the material to us by e-mail only the night before the wedding. It wasn't feasible for the DJ to make another slideshow in time for the dinner, so he played only mine. Jason's family was furious. His sister insulted mine, and his parents wore sour expressions and were uncommunicative for the entire rest of the night. They must have made their complaints and dissatisfaction clear to Jason and turned him against my family and me. He became sullen and uncommunicative during the rest of the reception, and I knew something was not right—maybe never would be right.

As I look back over these events, I ask myself how I could have gone through with it all. The anxiety I felt during the three weeks I spent in Lebanon dealing with Jason and his family as we planned our wedding must have shown clearly that marrying him was a mistake. The day before the wedding, my father told me I could just not do it—just not get married right away. But I was too sensitive to what people would say. So many people were coming to the wedding; so many plans had been made. I believed I had to go through with it. Call it societal pressure. Call it fear or pride. I don't know. I just could not stop the wedding. I went away from the reception to my wedding night without joy or sadness. The events of the previous seven months had wounded me. I felt as though I'd been married for one hundred years already. My only thought was to get back to America and begin our real life together. I believed that was the answer. I believed Jason could once again be the man I had met and fallen in love with—the man I had known for only the first month.

HONEYMOON

The first night of our honeymoon shocked me. We went to the Hotel Ehden, a beautiful hotel in the mountains in Lebanon, where I expected only love, passion, and kindness from Jason. Instead, he began our first night as man and wife by criticizing me for having spent money on expensive lingerie. He said I had been foolish to do that; it just was not necessary. On the second night, we argued again for a long time, mostly over the wedding reception. Suddenly, Jason announced that he was leaving; he would get away by taxi. He was angry because he felt my sister had insulted his sister over the stupid slideshow—the one she hadn't gotten to us in time to display pictures of Jason at the wedding. He was yelling loudly, and I begged him not to make a scene. The receptionist at the hotel was a school friend of mine. Not only did she hear the disturbance, but also the whole hotel heard him screaming. I was deeply upset and humiliated. I stayed in the room and let him go—worn out and tearful.

Jason returned a few hours later. His anger was spent. I don't remember if he said he was sorry, but I tried not to be angry and spiteful. I know now I had good reason to be both. At that time, though, I think I was covering my own shame and embarrassment. I was in denial and couldn't even gauge my feelings. Even by then, Jason had so convinced me that it was I who was wrong that I had no weapons to fight his angry words. So we went to bed and made love, but it was a cold kind of love. Then, we just slept until it was time to get up and continue our honeymoon trip. We spent three more days in Lebanon before going on to Jordan and the Dead Sea. For my part, these were tense and sad days. We didn't do any special sight-seeing or fun things, and Jason refused to spend time with my family. Jason seemed to be counting the minutes until he would be back in Jordan with his family. I was extremely careful about what I said and did. I never knew what would arouse his anger or cause him to humiliate me.

Even though it was our honeymoon, Jason was on the phone with his family every hour updating them on our every move. This made me confused and sad. Why would he take so much time with his family when this was such a special time for just us? But I didn't question him. This was our wedding trip. I loved him, wanted to love his family, and wanted to be a good wife. I believed this was the time to begin that very huge job.

When we left Lebanon for Jordan, my father, as he put us in the cab, told us to "always love one another, always respect one another. We will pray for you." I felt I was leaving all my security behind. I'd had many intimations of the negative side of Jason's character, and I was afraid—afraid of the kind of life that awaited me. But, I was determined that I was not going to give up; I would continue to believe things between us would get better and would work very hard to make that a reality. Still, I couldn't help crying in the cab, but I tried to keep this away from Jason. Even though he could see I was quiet and sad, he did nothing to comfort me. He was on his way to see his family; what could possibly be wrong?

We visited Jason's family five days after the wedding and spent three days with them. From the very first, I felt no true welcome. Jason's father showed me some warmth, but his mother was cold and distant. Even though we arrived quite late, probably near midnight, Jason's father immediately asked us if we wanted to eat. He took care of our luggage and sat with us to visit. In contrast, Jason's mother came to the door, briefly greeted us, and then went promptly back to bed.

All during our visit, Jason and his whole family spent much time arguing, shouting, and whispering behind closed doors; no one ever told me why. They rarely spoke to each other in a normal, conversational tone. The parents had many private conversations with Jason at which I was pointedly unwelcome. Though I didn't want to believe it then, I'm sure much of the conversation involved negative comments about my family and me. Later, Jason's mother said to me that she would have married him to anyone, just so long as he got married. I wasn't a real person to her, just the "anyone" she had settled for.

Jason's mother planned the days' outings; I was never consulted. No one asked me if there was anything I would like to see or anywhere I would like to go. Jason's family kept me closed in and away from Jason as though we weren't married. They would go off together and leave me behind. If I needed something, his parents would send me out with Jason's sister to get what I needed, rather than allow my husband to care for my needs. Jason made no objection to any of this. Throughout the visit, he did what they told him and let them do to me as they wished. It seemed that he was constantly trying to gain their approval, and though I couldn't understand it, it became clear to me that they were far more important to him than I was.

One pleasant thing happened on this visit. The extended family on my mother-in-law's side was invited for dinner. We had a meal together—a large and very good one—and I met aunts, uncles, and cousins, many of whom had not been at the wedding. The strange thing is that I immediately felt at ease with all of them. They were gracious and kind, positive and welcoming, and they really seemed to enjoy my company. They didn't show any of the negative traits that I had seen in Jason and his immediate family. This certainly got me to wondering. I felt good in this gathering, though, and it gave me hope that Jason could and would be more like this extended family if he got away from the influence of his parents. I am happy to say that I have kept in touch with quite a few of these people over the years. Sadly, Jason never did exhibit any of their appealing characteristics.

Conversation with Jason's family throughout the visit was almost impossible. When I introduced a topic, no one joined in. Often, one of the family, usually Jason's mother, would interrupt me and go on to something else. Sometimes, Jason's mother would just order her son around and make him do some menial chore like mopping the floor. It was as if she were telling me that she had complete control over him; I was nothing. Jason's response to her tended to confirm this. He did what she told him to do, and he would talk to her in a most subservient way—almost as if he were still a child. I wanted to make comments on this, but I refrained. That certainly would not have led to conversation of any good sort. The whole experience seemed odd and very wrong, but I thought since I didn't know them well yet, I might be misjudging them. I learned later that my impressions had been right, and Jason's parents eventually revealed themselves as a cruel, vengeful pair.

Jason's family could never be wrong. Whatever one of them said, the others agreed. If I disagreed, Jason would side with them. He did not defend me. Rather, he belittled me in front of his family. The smaller they could make me, the bigger they felt. I wanted to go out alone with Jason. I hoped we could take walks in the daytime and experience the exciting nightlife. He refused to do that. It was as if he really didn't want to be alone with me even though this was our honeymoon. I just didn't understand. What was I doing wrong? What was wrong with me? Through all this time, I felt deep shame. I think Jason and his family wanted me to feel that way. Still, I tried to hide the shame. I tried to act gracious and make it appear as though I was having a good time. I never showed my sadness or my tears. These feelings were foreign to me, and I knew they were irrational. I had done nothing wrong. I had nothing to feel ashamed of. Jason and his parents had created an atmosphere that excluded me and criticized me. Because I had never been in a similar situation, I couldn't see it for what it was. Their exclusion made me feel that I must be at fault—something must be the matter with me. So I began to believe that and began to lose more of myself, beginning with my self-confidence.

This trip marked another grave change in me. I began to lose respect for Jason. His subservience toward his mother and his refusal to stand up for me to his family created deep doubt in me, even resentment. I prayed these feelings would diminish. I had hopes that once we were out of there and away from the strong influence Jason's family had over him, we could begin a real married life together. Once we got back to the States, things would change. Jason would be as devoted to me as I was to him. Without his family, we could begin to build our own world—a good, peaceful, satisfying marriage—and make a family of our own. That's what Jason had promised me.

LIVING TOGETHER

Two weeks after the wedding, we returned to Jason's—now our—apartment in New Jersey. I was willing to make many sacrifices to make the marriage work. So that we could be together, it was necessary for me to quit two jobs in California, pay six thousand dollars in penalties for breaking my lease on a newly rented apartment, and leave all my friends. But Jason had to finish his residency in New Jersey, so that's where we lived. I was lucky to get a new position as a consultant, so we lived comfortably. In fact I picked up a second job a month latter and I had a very high paid income.

From the beginning, though, Jason increasingly treated me without respect and quickly fell into a pattern of directing all my actions. He told me what water I could drink, where I could eat, and how much money I could spend. He didn't even want me to treat myself to a Starbucks' coffee. He was constantly talking about money and how we couldn't spend it. I cooked dinners every day and packed lunches for Jason. We never ordered food in, and even when I cooked a good meal, Jason would eat it standing, showing no respect for me and the meal I had prepared. It was as though he didn't want to give up the habits he had when he was a single man—a third-year resident with very little time to eat. I tried incessantly to get him to sit down and share our meal, but he consistently refused. He never appreciated the effort I took to prepare food for him. Having a dinner out together was no pleasure either; Jason commented only on the price of the meal. Then, he would tell me how much the meal cost and how much I should appreciate him for spending that much on me.

He also became obsessed with what he considered the horrifying situation of my education and automobile loans. He demanded that I put all of the money I earned toward paying off these debts. His obsession over money became very troubling—and humiliating. To keep peace, I allowed all of my earnings to go toward paying off my loans, and I paid them in full the first year that we were married. It was an awful sacrifice, but I was willing to make it to keep the peace and stay married.

Jason had ways other than angry outbursts to keep me in line. When I did what he asked without complaining or talking back to him, he could be sweet, even kind. He would bring home flowers, tell me how much he loved me—the beautiful, sweet, intelligent girl he had married. Then we would make love, and all seemed good again. But all this was a way of encouraging me to be more submissive and continue to lose my identity. All I had to do was follow his directions, do what he wanted, give him complete control over me, and he would make everything good. Today, it's impossible to imagine that I could ever have been taken in by such a scam!

During our time in New Jersey, I began to see a definite insecurity in him as well as a kind of secretiveness that were most disturbing. Out of the blue one day, he told me that he couldn't communicate face-to-face with me; he wanted me to write all my thoughts and answers to his questions in e-mails. I'd never heard of anything like this before and thought it was very strange and ridiculous. I see now that he wanted to document everything about our lives. I didn't know why at the time, but I fell for it. During this time, he shouted commands at me and provoked me and waited for my angry answers in e-mail. Whenever we argued, Jason would pull out his phone and force me to repeat what I had said so he could tape my words. This was one of his ways to abuse me and shut me up. Although I began to become more and more concerned and confused, I simply did not know how to respond, and I didn't tell anyone about Jason's strange demands. I continued to do as he asked me to do even though I could make no sense of it. I knew that Jason shared everything with his parents, and I was afraid he would find a way to use what I said against me. He was a master at taking things out of context and making the most innocent things I said or did appear mean and malicious. It was best that I just say nothing.

Computers figured in our lives in another odd way. One day I was looking at pictures on Jason's phone. Several were of very attractive women. Curious about them, I opened his text messages and learned that less than a month before we started to date, he had been sending romantic messages to other women—the same messages that he had sent to me. I then found e-mails that Jason had sent to nearly forty women when he was looking for a wife. He had proposed to multiple women, including a woman who didn't want to relocate. Not surprisingly, he had never told me this. He had a list of questions that he would ask those he corresponded with. They seemed like interview questions aimed at finding a trophy wife. After reading these messages, I felt sad and disappointed. Was I just another of Jason's "interviewees"? Had he ever been sincerely in love with just me?

I thought back to my early conversations with Jason and began to think I was right, that he had interviewed me, too. When I thought we were just getting to know one another, he would ask me things like, "Would you correct me in public if I was wrong and your friend was right? Whose side would you take if your parents wanted us to baptize our children but I didn't? Would you put me first before our kids? Would you relocate with me anywhere, even if I wanted to go back to the Middle East? Would you go with me to any church?" I didn't think too much about these questions at the time, but it did seem that Jason had some sort of agenda. He asked one or two of these questions every day until, as he said, he allowed himself to love me. To him, love didn't come naturally; he could only let himself love someone who met all of his qualifications. After all the interrogation, he had decided that he was not attaching himself to the wrong person. I guess the interview was successful.

Jason's computer dating had one very sad effect on his own family. While we were dating, we learned that his sister had been engaged, but the engagement was abruptly broken off after a short time largely due to Jason's involvement with his sister's future sister-in-law. When I asked him about this, Jason told me that he had been dating his sister's future sister-in-law even while he was dating me, but he swore he hadn't made her any promises. When his sister's fiancé found out that Jason was planning to marry me, he got very angry and broke his engagement with Jason's sister. In Jordanian culture, what Jason had done was seen as dishonorable to the other family, and he felt he could not marry the sister of a man who had committed such dishonor. In a sense, the brother's argument was, "How do you play my sister like that and make her promises and then dump her for another woman?"

It seemed to torment Jason that he had caused this breakup. At the time, I sympathized with him and told him that it wasn't his fault. But knowing what I know now, I think differently. Since I know that he was speed dating and romancing different women simultaneously, I have no doubt that he played that poor girl as well. He wanted to keep his options open. He wasn't looking for love; he was shopping for a decent, educated woman. The funny thing is that even though he was looking for intelligent and independent women, those were the two qualities he hated most in me.

I tried hard to talk to Jason, especially about the things I thought were hurting our marriage. I didn't attack his personality traits, but I would calmly try to explain my viewpoint, for example, why I preferred to drink bottled water. He always responded with harsh criticism, "You don't need bottled water; tap water is fine. You're just too particular. You waste our money." I simply didn't know how to respond. I'd never been attacked in this way before. I'd never had to justify such a seemingly insignificant choice. But it wasn't insignificant to Jason; nothing I did was too small for his scrutiny. After all, everything I did was now part of his world, and he was determined to control every part of it.

A curious incident occurred in the second month of our marriage and must have been prompted by Jason monitoring my e-mail. Before I was married, I had sent an e-mail to a male friend I used to work with. This man had told me he cared for me. I sent an e-mail explaining I was in love with Jason. I told him he should marry someone else because I had already chosen my path. It was a pity e-mail, which is typical for any girl to write when she feels bad for a guy she doesn't really care for. But Jason's response was more than excessive. I was out driving when my Blackberry showed me someone was accessing my e-mail account. Fearing that Jason would criticize me for something in my e-mails, I rushed home. When I tried to get in our apartment, he grabbed me, screamed at me, and pushed me out the door. This was the first time that his abuse was physical, and I was horrified. I begged him to let me in and, finally, he did, though he continued shouting at me and pushing me around the apartment.

I was so distraught over the pushing and screaming that I fell to my knees and started wailing. I moved from side to side and hit my head on the floor. I didn't understand how this could be happening to me. Jason paid no attention to my condition. He called my family and told them I was a whore and a cheater and he wouldn't believe anything I said since we never communicate in a normal way. It was always Jason attacking and me trying to defend myself. My parents took his side to calm things down. Jason apparently had convinced them I had acted inappropriately, and they urged me to stop doing that. They tried to convince Jason that I did not have bad intentions, and had acted in error. Above all, they wanted to find ways to keep us together

I was traumatized because he had humiliated me in front of my family and he had hurt me physically. My parents called often, and for a while I wouldn't speak to them because I was so embarrassed. When I finally did answer their calls, I told them Jason and I just had an argument on the night he called them, but everything was fine now. Then I moved quickly on to other topics. I desperately did not want my parents or anyone else to know how Jason treated me in the privacy of our home.

Some hours later, both Jason and I had calmed down. Just like many times before when he had been angry, Jason told me how special I was and how much he loved me. It was hard not to believe him; I kept hoping that our marriage would one day be a happy one. I recovered from this incident and kept pushing forward.

It became a pattern: Jason would get angry and mistreat me, and then he would apologize and tell me he loved me. I would become angry and hurt, but I always forgave him. I couldn't stop believing things between us would improve. Later, though, every time we had an argument, Jason would mention the man to whom I had sent that e-mail and say very cruelly that I should have married him. He never let go of this e-mail and never truly forgave me for what his mind told him was a grave transgression. Our communication continued to be through e-mail. If I was sad, if I was happy, if I had an opinion, if I purchased something, if I had plans—all these things I had to tell Jason in e-mails. Jason was obsessed with documenting things; he made me give him receipts for everything I purchased. Every time we argued or any time I said something he didn't like, he would write it in an e-mail to himself or to me so that he could always refer to it. Any time I didn't do the dishes, he put that in an e-mail. When I made a sandwich for him, he would write that I didn't care about his health because of the amount of cholesterol in the sandwich. Though these were minor things, he used them as reasons to rage against me.

He needed the reassurance of this documentation to justify himself for his treatment of me. But he never cared about the e-mails I sent telling him I loved him; those he disregarded altogether. I have no doubt that, for the four years of our marriage, he shared all this with his parents to give them all the details of our life together. It was only his take on that life, though; I never got to share my side.

Our First Christmas

Another sad and disappointing occurrence happened on our first Christmas together. The Christmas season intensified my love, and I forgot the unhappy things that had happened in the previous months. I loved Jason and wanted him to be happy on this special day. I left work early on Christmas Eve to buy Jason many gifts, including new clothing that he needed, with my own money. (It's important to note that I only ever used my own money. I never had access to his money or accounts.) I was very happy in anticipation of this special time together. I wrapped the gifts and decorated them and put out rose petals with wine and candles. How could I have anticipated how short-lived my happiness would be?

Instead of the joy I had anticipated, I received sorrow and rejection. When Jason came home and saw what I had done, he screamed at me. He spat out that he hated surprises, and he insisted that I shouldn't spend money on gifts. His parents had taught his family that they didn't need to buy gifts just because it was Christmas. He wanted me to learn that same lesson and be like his parents. While he was calling me materialistic and superficial, he made me unwrap the gifts one by one and tried to make me return them. I didn't do that, though, because his clothing was old and tattered, and I knew he needed new clothes. Jason did use them. Once he had made his point and belittled me, the actual clothes weren't important.

Our First Valentine

On our first Valentine's Day, anything but love ruled the day. I had a work meeting in New York that day and ran into some friends, one of whom was a man. So I called Jason and told him my friends said "hi." Jason knew that one of them was male, and he was very angry and wasted no time in telling me so. I was filled with fear on the train returning to New Jersey. Jason was waiting at home for me. He looked at me so angrily and fiercely that I feared he would beat me. He shouted loudly and pushed me out the door. Once again, I had to beg to be let in. He did so, but he kept up the screaming and verbal abuse, calling me a liar and a whore, until he had worn himself out. Then, he calmed down and wanted to kiss and make up. I thought the incident was over.

How wrong I was! That same night we had a Valentine party to go to in New Jersey. My uncle had bought us tickets, and we were to pick up his wife and all meet up at the party. Jason began right away talking about my meeting in New York that day and about my friend. Throughout the forty-five-minute drive, Jason acted like a madman. He repeatedly slammed his fist on the dashboard and against the doors and also hit me against the door. His only words were to curse me and threaten to drag me by my hair in front of my family. I cried and begged him not to hurt me and not to embarrass me. I pleaded with him to stop the car. The only place we saw was a Laundromat, so he stopped there and I got out. I went into the building, sat on a bench, and cried. I was very scared of this new violence. I didn't know what was going to happen.

Finally, Jason dragged me back into the car, and we arrived at my uncle's house. Jason was still hitting me as we sat in the car. I knew my uncle's wife saw us because I could see her standing at the window. I again begged Jason to stop what he was doing, and I said I would do anything to make him stop. I'm almost ashamed to tell of the humiliating thing he wanted. He made me kiss his shoes over and over again before he would stop screaming. We stayed in the car, and Jason lifted first one leg then the other. He made me bend down as he held his feet toward me. That seemed humiliation enough, but it wasn't the end.

When my aunt got in the car, Jason started all over again with his jealous ravings about my being in love with other men and what he thought was my disrespect for him. My aunt told Jason that she knew all my friends and that I had no special relationship with any other man. He insisted that she was wrong. I just wished the earth would open up and swallow me. Throughout the drive to the party, I sat shivering, sweating, and grinding my teeth.

At the party, Jason completely changed. He wanted to dance. He smiled and acted as though nothing had happened. He even bought me a rose. I was shocked at this behavior, this mystifying change in personality. Jason was calm when we got into the car and stayed that way for a short time. But soon, he started in again on my unfaithfulness with other men. Again, he called me names and shouted that I was a bad person. I'm sure it was then that I started telling myself, "This is not happening. Jason cannot possibly be that aggressive. It's not possible that he has no shame." I went into denial, I'm sure, and I started to build a wall around myself to keep from going crazy, shutting down, or breaking down. I must have convinced myself I could be safe if I only stayed behind that wall. That was how, after the party was over, I was still able to sleep with him and make love.

My wall was in place, and I was safe. I'll never forget our first Valentine's Day, though. It was a truly traumatizing event, one of so many I lived through with him. That day I concluded that Jason was just an abnormal type of man that you could never please. Unbelievably, I thought I would be able to live with that.

Our First Visit to Jordan
after a Year of Marriage

In the summer after our marriage, Jason and I planned a visit to both our families. First, we went to Jordan to visit with Jason's family. I went bearing special gifts of clothes, jewelry, and accessories that I gave from my heart. I hoped and prayed this would be a healing visit and all the unpleasantness that had happened at the wedding would be forgotten. I wanted Jason's family to like me—to love me—and I wanted to be able to show them that I truly loved them. That wasn't to be.

One day I had Lasik surgery on my eyes and was in Jason's room with a headache and very itchy eyes. As part of my recovery, I had to wear special goggles after the surgery too. I told Jason I wasn't able to leave the bedroom to come out to dinner that evening. Rather than treating me with concern, he started yelling at me: "My mom made a special meal and you don't want to eat! You have a black heart! You are mean. You are disrespectful and ungrateful!" I knew the whole family could hear these awful words, and I begged Jason to calm down. Now, I was ashamed to leave the room, and I was certain I wouldn't be welcomed at dinner. For the rest of the evening, I stayed in my room; no one showed concern for me. Instead, Jason went into his parents' room, and they locked the door. I knew they were talking about me and not in any kind or good way, focusing, I'm sure, on how little I appreciated them.

One day, Jason's sister offered to take me for a pedicure. I thanked her but suggested we wait a week so that the pedicure would be fresh for my trip back to Lebanon. This upset her, and she complained to Jason. He came to me and said, "You don't appreciate anything my family does for you." My simple suggestion had caused such a stir that I decided to go for the pedicure that day and be done with it for the sake of peace. With that family, there was no compromise.

During the whole visit, I felt like an orphan. One day, Jason's mother told me, "Mouch hilou el nakad." ("It's not nice to be a nag.") I stayed quiet and didn't talk back. Jason never took me out. If I needed something, even something as simple as shampoo, Jason put his sister or mother in control. They took me to get what I needed, but they were never happy about it; they made me feel that I was a burden. At that time, I was too timid and shy to make any demands on Jason. He left me hanging without support. He always disappeared when it was time to focus on me. My emotions were disregarded and I was always in an emotional loneliness. Of course, I didn't really know his family, and it was uncomfortable for me to be with them without him. Being in this situation and not having Jason's help and support had a horrible effect on me. The insecurity and instability of that family made me feel insecure and unstable. I felt I could not trust Jason when we were near his family, and he never stood up for me against them. These feelings diminished after the trip, but they recurred when his parents called or visited us.

First Lebanon Trip after
a Year of Marriage

I was very happy to leave Jason's family and head for Lebanon. But how quickly my happiness turned to despair. I thought we would spend the days with my parents, going places, enjoying things, and loving just being together. Jason had other ideas. He didn't want to spend one minute with my family.

Jason and I spent much time away from my parents' home either out by ourselves or sometimes with my sister or cousin. He was always arrogant; he cursed me in private and embarrassed me. I don't know how I hid this embarrassment—almost shame—from my parents. But I kept smiling and making the best excuses I could for not spending time with them. Whenever he got me alone, Jason told me he did not want even to be around my parents. He didn't want my parents to come out with us to restaurants because he was afraid he'd be expected to pay. That would never happen, of course; my dad is more than generous. We were raised to be generous, and that's how we treat our guests and families. Jason seemed to be the only one who didn't know and appreciate that; he would deny anything done for him. He would not take gifts my father offered him. Somehow he needed to feel superior to my family, and accepting gifts from them would lessen that sense of superiority. Later, Jason's mother complained to me that my family didn't feed him or take him places in Lebanon. These were all lies Jason fed her so that he could look like a victim to his family.

After five days, Jason returned to the United States, and I stayed with my parents for two more weeks. While I remained in Lebanon, Jason called me and texted me what seemed like a hundred times a day, telling me how wrong I was to have stayed there and not returned with him. He not only created issues of contention, but he also brought up things from the past—what he thought were wrong, bad things I had done. He gave me not a single day of peace with my family during this visit. Many times after one of his insulting remarks, all I could do was cry. Then, I had to dry my eyes and pretend that I was happy. At times, I didn't think I could do it, but I kept making the effort. I truly believed no one knew.

I can't imagine how my first visit home as a married woman could have been worse. I never told my parents or my sisters how Jason acted or what he said to me in private. They might have known, but they are not the kind of people who interfere. They wanted the best for me and for Jason, too. They must have thought that marriage was just a difficult adjustment for us and prayed for things to get better as we went forward and made our lives together.

Although I was sad to leave my parents once again, I was ready to return home. I certainly did not want to go back to Jordan. But without consulting me, Jason and his father had arranged that I would spend a day in Jordan before taking the plane home. So I first flew from Lebanon to Jordan. Immediately after Jason's dad picked me up, Jason's mother insisted that we go to a restaurant. I wasn't feeling well and barely picked at the food, which made his mother angry. That evening, although I still felt ill, Jason's mother badgered me to go to their church with his sister, even though I had no interest in becoming a participant in the Church of Christ. It was another incident that showed me his mother wanted to change me—to make me more like her.

The next day, Jason's mother acted most strangely. She took me aside. She was crying, which upset me greatly, but what she said upset me more. "Divorce is bad, ugly," she said. And then, "Always try to work things out." I was dumbfounded. Had Jason talked with her about divorce? I certainly hadn't done that, and I hadn't told anyone I had reason to want a divorce. Jason must have discussed this with her. Was he, then, really thinking of divorce? During our marriage, he had repeatedly threatened to divorce me, saying he couldn't live this way anymore. Then he would tell me that he had only good memories of our time together. I must have mumbled something in reply. I left there with a sinking heart, sad and confused. Whatever Jason's mother was concerned about, it wasn't me. Her concern, as always, was only for her son.

Jason's father drove me to the airport that morning. I tried again to be close to him by treating him as I would treat my own father. In my culture, asking a close relative for assistance is a sign of trust and respect. I asked him for a Jordanian dollar because I thought I would have to use Jordanian currency in the airport. He answered me curtly that I could use US dollars. It appeared as if I was just trying to get him to give me money. He treated me like Jason would treat me. Once again, I was humiliated by Jason's family. I had no hope of ever getting close to any of them. Later I found out that Jason cheated on me the first time during our first year of marriage and I always wondered why he asked me throughout the marriage about my tolerance for unfaithfulness.

We Move to the Midwest

As Jason was finishing his residency, it was time for him to find a permanent position. One month after we were married, we went to a rural Midwestern area for his interview with the local major hospital. We were both shocked when we saw the main city where Jason would work. It was very small, so different from the cities both Jason and I had lived in. Neither of us liked it at all, though the beautiful autumn colors and the cordiality of the people we met reassured us somewhat.

Jason and I discussed this potential move. I tried to talk about the quality of life we might have—or not have—there. His focus, though, was on the money. He was offered an excellent salary and benefits and help in sponsoring for his green card. (He didn't need the green card, however, because he became eligible when he married me.) These things took precedence over any objection I brought up. It was obvious that he wanted to take the position he had been offered and that he expected me to be the compliant, supportive wife. Although I believed this was not a good decision for us, I agreed to the move. I know people initially need to make sacrifices in marriage so they have a better chance of getting the things they really want later. Thinking this way made it easier for me to go along with Jason's wishes.

It was difficult to find a place that I liked and where I felt safe. Jason didn't seem to care and hurried me through all the house hunting. I found one house that was pleasant and in a safe area but not particularly close to the hospital.

Although the rental rate was quite reasonable, Jason pestered the realtor for a discount. Even though he would be making very good money, he couldn't hide his stinginess. We moved there toward the end of our first year of marriage. And *every day*, Jason complained to me about having to drive thirty-five minutes to work. What made me happy about our location just incited his anger. My primary concern was safety because, at that time, Jason was working only night shifts, and I was afraid to be alone at night. It was as if my desire to be in a safe, pleasant place was much less important than his convenience in getting to work.

It was difficult at first for me to make friends, and I was sad and lonely for quite some time. Fortunately, I was able to continue my work as a remote employee, so I didn't feel as completely alone and isolated as I could have in a new location. Jason worked so much that I didn't meet many of his colleagues or their wives. It took me about a year to build relationships with some of the other physicians' wives, especially those from the Middle East.

Our home life was rarely pleasant. Jason constantly badgered me because everything ticked him off: the weather, the TV, the dishes, the carpet, the way I talked, the way I walked, the way I breathed, the way I cooked, the way I cleaned, and so on. He was constantly judgmental about everything I did. He gave me no real say in the running of our home; he needed to control everything. He obsessed about food and monitored everything that I threw out. If I did throw something out, he would look in the garbage and even retrieve expired food or a rotten banana, which he would then eat. He would insist that we eat expired food and take expired medication, claiming that expiration dates didn't mean anything.

I knew these habits were carried over from the way his parents had raised him. In a rare moment of emotional intimacy, Jason confided that his mother would tell him to "clean out the refrigerator." This meant that he should eat up anything that was left. Jason proudly told me that his mother named him the "vacuum cleaner." I felt bad for him. I kept my true feelings to myself and showed him only respect. There was nothing I could do to detach him from these old, destructive habits.

Even with all these trials, I believed that I sincerely and genuinely loved Jason. I wanted to build him up. I wanted him to be the very best he could be. It was impossible for me to convince him of my faith in him or my support. He accused me of having neither. Yet, a few times in weak moments, he said to me, "I don't know how you have the patience to deal with me. May God help you." Ultimately, though, his relatives were the only ones that he believed in. They were the only ones who could love and support him as he needed. He didn't understand that what appeared as love and support could really be manipulation and control.

No one knew about our suffocating and unhappy home life. I always made a point of smiling broadly and being pleasant when I was out of the home. Everyone thought Jason and I were a great, good-looking couple. Jason proudly told his colleagues at the hospital that I was a "trophy wife." He felt this made him look good. When I finally met some of Jason's colleagues at a Christmas party in his first year of work, Jason treated me very well in front of them. There wasn't the slightest hint of the discord that was ever present in our home. I was always glad for the respite from the constant arguing, but I hated the hypocrisy.

By this time, I was beginning to make many friends. I loved entertaining and hosted dinner parties from time to time. Jason always criticized me for this. He hated to have people over and always made preparations difficult. He told me not to buy so much; we didn't need so many (and such expensive) appetizers and so on. An hour or so before the guests arrived, though, Jason's mood would change. He became anxious that everything was just right. Sometimes he would make me wash the plates or glasses again, insisting that they were not clean. He wanted, as always, to look very good in front of people.

When the guests came, Jason would sit and socialize with them while I took care of their needs. I tried not to notice too much, but I always felt Jason puffed himself up before our guests. He had to be the center of attention—just like his mother. He knew everything and talked constantly. I sometimes interrupted his conversations to let a guest get a word in, but shortly after, Jason would take over again.

At other times, Jason tried to keep us from doing things I enjoyed. If we were invited to dinner or a party and I was happy about the invitation, Jason would find a reason for us not to go. If I expressed interest in a movie or play, he would say it wasn't worth our time. After this happened many times, I learned that if I pretended not to be interested, he would insist that we attend whatever the function was. I'm certainly not proud of putting on such a pretense. I was learning Jason's ways of manipulation that had not been part of my makeup before.

Jason always seemed well-assembled and self-assured and then he would pull the rug from under my feet leaving me fearful, disgusted, bored and in tears. He was always too busy painting the perfect image of himself as a husband and a father to his family for whom he goes for approval daily that he didn't have time to work on being one. He constantly fished for compliments and favors from anyone he can prey on, and wanted me to put him on an undeserved pedestal. Jason demanded explanations for the simplest matters as if he knew nothing about common sense, and he always felt entitled to protect his ego through attacks and distractions. He never empathized with me nor is he capable of empathy one of many reasons he treated me like an object, a trophy, a property and never like a lady.

A Significant Trip

In the fall of our first year in the Midwest, I had to go on a business trip to California. By that time, I knew Jason was insanely jealous, and he would imagine that I was going to meet a lover. I asked Jason to go with me so that he would know I wasn't going to meet up with another man. He agreed to come, but I still couldn't avoid his hostile behavior.

A simple action on my part sent Jason into a rage. Thinking it would be helpful after we landed, I went ahead and made arrangements for our rental car while Jason was in the airport restroom. I texted him to tell him what was going on and where I would meet him. Jason blew up. I don't know if he felt insecure, out of place, or just angry that we were in California, a place that he knew I loved. I do know that he couldn't bear not being in control, and my simple action of arranging for a car apparently took control away from him. Also, it was a sign of independence, which Jason did not want me to have. He called me and said that he would not meet me; he intended to take a flight back to St. Louis immediately. People were expecting to see both of us, and I begged him not to embarrass me yet again. Once more, I was forced to plead with him, to beg him for simple courtesy.

Finally, after more than an hour of frantic pleading on the phone, Jason allowed me to pick him up and get on our way. We headed toward our hotel; Jason was sullen, and I could tell an explosion was coming. We were driving on a large, busy California highway, and I felt horribly frightened. And then it happened. As I was driving, Jason started hitting me, slapping my face, and pulling my hair. He screamed that I had done wrong by leaving him in the restroom—I should have stayed and waited for him. I had no right to leave him there alone. I was selfish and thoughtless. By the time we reached the hotel, I was a mess and in much pain. The beating in the car left my arms bruised, and to hide the bruises, I had to wear sweaters everywhere we went even though it was hot summer weather there. People at work asked questions about that, but I was able to make up excuses, though they probably weren't convincing.

During the days while I was at work, Jason took the car and went sightseeing. The first morning after the incident in the car, he said nothing about it; he simply accepted my suggestions about what he could go to see that day and left. Jason was opportunistic; it didn't matter that he had so recently beat me. It didn't matter that I was working and he was able to go sightseeing. He had no hesitation about taking advantage of the situation. Sometime during the day, he sent me a text: "Wish you were with me." At first, I was angry—how could he be such a hypocrite? But as usual, I quickly recovered hope. I told myself that when we got back home we'd be able to resolve our issues, and Jason would once again show that he loved me.

In the evenings, my employers and friends wanted to take us out to dinner. Jason usually declined, but he did attend once or twice. This was awkward for me because Jason's social skills were limited, and I never knew what he would say or do. I never relaxed during these outings. Sadly, even pleasant evenings were marred by a deep anxiety that something would go wrong or Jason would get angry about an imagined insult.

I think it was during that trip that I finally took a hard look at myself. I had changed so very much. Once open and trusting, I had become very much closed and fearful. Once confident, I now cringed when Jason criticized me; I had no idea how to fight back or even stand up for myself. And that lack of confidence in myself carried over into my professional life. I had become fearful of what my superiors would say to me, constantly thinking that I must have done something wrong. I was always ready to apologize or justify myself like I was forced to do with Jason. I walked on eggshells at home and now at work.

With these realizations came another: I did not have to accept what Jason did to me. Jason had worked hard to change me, but I'm the one who allowed him to do it. I thought I had good motives in always forgiving him for what he did and said to me. I wanted a happy marriage. I wanted to be a good wife. But now I saw I would get neither of these things by docilely accepting emotional and physical abuse. I needed to stand up for myself if I could. I vowed at least to try to fight back. I vowed to try to find the woman I used to be. I knew doing these things would be very difficult, but I also knew I had to try.

Jason always hid behind a false bravado, masking his insecurities and unmet childhood needs. He was chastised for miner behaviors and only loved when he made his mother look good and proud. Till this date, Jason can't survive without his parents' approval and their reassurance that they care for him. This is where they have him manipulated and under their controls; And I thought I can break into this circle. Jason was never shown how to walk in someone else's shoes and grew with almost no social awareness and responsibility. He was beaten with shame and criticism and I was the surrogate victim her wanted to revenge from. He torn me down and built me up at his convenience and the more he controlled my mind the more he lied and demanded.

PREGNANCY

Although I hadn't told my parents very much about my problems with Jason, my mother sensed that ours was by no means a perfect marriage. Once when I was talking to my mother, she urged me to have a child. She believed that would change things for Jason and me. Perhaps fatherhood would make him more compassionate and peaceful. When I did get pregnant, Jason made no effort to express joy or any positive emotion. We had been quarreling more and more, and it seemed nothing, not even a baby, would bring joy to our home. Jason confessed that day that his mother attempted abortion with his brother and he miraculously survived. It felt as he was indirectly encouraging me for one; I was puzzled at his interjection. This baby was my dream come true and the day I knew I conceived Lauren was the best day of my life.

My pregnancy did not change Jason; it seemed to make him more irritable and quarrelsome. If he criticized me for something and I tried to defend myself, he would carry on yelling for hours. He would take out his frustration by hitting things in the house: walls, tables, doors. He would come close behind me and breathe down my neck, shouting louder all the time. He became more jealous of my friends and didn't want me to see people. I wonder if he was jealous of our unborn child—jealous that I might love the baby more than I loved him.

When I was one month pregnant, Jason was preparing our taxes. He confronted me about what he said was twenty thousand dollars missing from my income. He had itemized all my income and accounted for all I had spent, but insisted money was missing and that I had secretly sent it all to my family. He refused to understand that I had spent money paying off my car and school loans, decorating the house, and providing for necessities. His only contribution to home maintenance was paying the rent and utilities. Out of my income, I supplied all the rest, including clothing and preparing for the baby's arrival. But he insisted I had stolen the money for my own purposes and to send money to my family. All these senseless accusations.

Shortly after this incident, one of my sisters came for a three-week visit to pursue academic interests. Jason was angry all the time during her visit, and I was afraid of him. He hated having any of my family in our home, and he made my sister's stay particularly bitter. He made me wake him up when she had her meals so that he could see how much she ate. He called from work to ask what she was doing. He complained that she was taking too long in the shower. He complained that whenever my family came we had to spend too much money. It particularly bothered Jason that my sister's boyfriend sent her gifts while she was with us. He thought that was a bad example for me, that I would expect to receive gifts from him now.

My sister was shocked at my appearance. She said I looked oppressed. She said my demeanor had changed. I talked in a very soft voice (to keep from annoying Jason), and it seemed like I was walking on eggshells, afraid of everything around me. I had stopped caring about my appearance; my clothes were untidy, I needed a haircut, and I wore no makeup. I was scared; I didn't want her to know what was going on between Jason and me. I didn't want to trouble her, and I didn't want her to report to my parents. I was afraid if they knew, they would become ill. So I made a huge effort to appear normal and do fun things with my sister. Jason called and texted me continually while she was with me. He wanted to know what we were doing, what we were eating, what we were spending. When he was home, he would ask me via text message to go into the bedroom with him where he would continue the questions and let me know how much he disapproved when my sister opened the refrigerator, used our iPad, watched TV, or used too much water for her shower. I did the best I could to cover up Jason's behavior, but I'm sure my sister suspected that all was not well.

During my pregnancy, Jason pushed me against the wall many times. One time, I insulted Jason by telling him, "You are like the woman in the house." He called my father and told him I said Jason is a woman. He must have said outrageous things about me because my dad then called me often, obviously very worried. He told me not to say things like that to Jason. My mother, when I talked with her, was always choked up or crying. Not only was I miserably embarrassed, I was also fearful for my parents—fearful that they would become sick over my situation. Every time my mother or father called me, their concern was obvious. They could not help wondering just what was going on between Jason and me. Was I unhappy? Was I ill? Were Jason and I going to get a divorce? And still, I told them nothing. I couldn't bring myself to share my troubles with them, and I continued to hope for better days. Jason wasn't worried about any of us, though. He even said that he was going to call my father and tell him about our "issues" so that he would have a heart attack and die. Unbelievable!

The trauma I felt from this threatening situation, from Jason's violence, made me ill. The day after I insulted him and he threatened my father, we had another argument. Jason grabbed me by my face and pushed me out of the house. I fell down and felt a very sharp pain in my abdomen. I drove myself to my obstetrician, who insisted that I needed to go to the emergency room. I was afraid to do that because I knew Jason would be angry that I went there without consulting him, but I had no choice. I believed that I was having a miscarriage, so I drove myself to the emergency room.

After I was examined, I was reassured that I was not having a miscarriage. It appears that the pain resulted from stress over the argument I had with Jason. I was given pain medication, and the nurse asked me if I felt safe to go home. I said yes, but I was horrified by the implication in her words. Had I become *that* woman—an abused woman? I just couldn't face it. It was a huge mistake to say yes, I could go home with Jason, but, still, I didn't want to hurt Jason's reputation; I didn't want to humiliate him at the very hospital that employed him.

But he didn't care about humiliating me. When they called him to the ER and the nurse left, all he did was belittle me. He was in no way upset because I was in pain or might have had a miscarriage. His only concern was the money it cost for me to be treated in the ER. He raged that what he called my "emotional issues" made him pay one hundred dollars for a deductible charge. I often wonder if any of his coworkers overheard his words or saw his actions that day.

Weeks later, Jason and I got into another argument, and I could do nothing to make him stop raging at me. I cowered on the floor, vomiting, shaking, and panting from fear. This had become typical. When Jason was with me, he didn't communicate; he attacked me in my face and scared me. I learned to stay where I was until the screaming stopped. That was the safest thing for the baby I was carrying and for me. In his rage, Jason didn't care for the health of the baby. All he cared about was getting his message across, and he only stopped shouting when he was done with his speeches.

Jason's cruelty wasn't limited to when he was angry. When we were in the car together, he would slam the breaks repeatedly until I got nauseated and vomited. He wouldn't stop the car and let me get out when this happened. He wanted to show me that he had power over me, even to make me sick. He knew how nauseated I got while riding in cars, and he kept slamming on the breaks. He'd ask, "Are you vomiting yet?" He kept this horrible behavior up until we arrived at our destination. Remembering those awful times, I can't imagine why I stayed with this man who was not only violent and selfish and didn't know love, but who also didn't care for the well-being of his wife or child.

I had only a brief time of relief in my nine months of pregnancy. When I was seven months pregnant, Jason went to his sister's wedding in Jordan. One of my sisters came to be with me while he was gone. It was such a peaceful time for me. No arguments, no abuse. My sister and I just enjoyed one another and talked of the wonderful future I would have with my baby. I was also very glad for my sister's help with the cooking and cleaning. Although I was sick during most of my pregnancy and worked two full-time remote jobs as a consultant, Jason would not let me hire anyone to help with daily chores.

Jason's Brother Visits

Very close to the time our baby was due, we had a three-week visit from Jason's younger brother. Jason knew he was coming, but he didn't tell me until the day his brother arrived. He was a typical sixteen-year old, and it wasn't much fun to have him around, especially in my condition. He was extremely moody and mostly isolated himself in the bedroom. But I did manage to take him shopping for clothes, and he appreciated that. Then I heard him talking to his mother. It seemed that she was giving him directions on what to say and do while he was with us. It sounded to me like he was with us to report back to her on what was happening in our home. His mother's jealousy may also have been a motivation for his visit. It seemed that whenever one of my relatives visited, shortly after that one of Jason's relatives would come. My mother-in-law apparently wanted to make sure that my relatives weren't treated any better than Jason's relatives were.

LABOR PAIN

My labor was a horror scene. We went to the hospital—Jason, my visiting mother, and I. Jason showed his callousness by deciding it would take some time before the baby came, and he left to buy an iPhone. That time he was gone at least two hours. (He left often and for hours at a time during my twenty-four hour labor.) He came back with food for my mother, who wasn't hungry and politely declined the offered meal. As I painfully labored, Jason complained to me that my mom was refusing the sandwich he had gotten for her. He thought it was more important for my mother to eat what he had brought her than for her to attend her daughter and soon-to-arrive grandchild!

My labor was long and complicated, and I had to give birth to our daughter, Lauren, via a cesarean section. As I recovered, Jason kept nagging me that my mom was a burden staying at the hospital with us. He never cared about my pain; all he cared about was ordering more free food from the hospital kitchen so he didn't have to go get food for himself. I had just had major surgery, but he treated me as though I had done nothing special. I wished that he would show at least some tenderness toward me in these special moments. Instead, he couldn't stop being authoritative and insensitive.

He showed all the consideration for his mother that he didn't show to me. As I was coming out of surgery, he had his mother on Skype in my recovery room despite my wish for privacy. He shared every moment with his family instead of focusing on his wife and newborn daughter. Once again, it was all about him and his family. To me, this was a private moment, not one to parade in front of his family.

After Lauren was born, I remained in the hospital for five days. The days were difficult; I was in constant pain and struggling to be able to feed my child. Finally, I was well enough to go home. A male nurse came to discharge me. He shared that he had seven kids, and one was named Lauren—like our Lauren. I was so happy and overwhelmed to have Lauren that I began chatting with the nurse about the coincidence. Even this innocuous incident caused upheaval.

Later that day at home, I was breastfeeding Lauren, and Jason started slamming and rocking the bed as he shouted at me. He accused me of falling in love with the male nurse and again called me a whore. Somehow, I managed to drown out his hateful words in my happiness with Lauren. I could think only of her, and that protected me for a time from Jason's hurtfulness. I stayed with this man and kept hoping for a miracle. It is sad to say that his abuse increased.

AFTER LAUREN'S BIRTH

My dreams of having a better life with Jason now that we had a child of our own were quickly dispelled. He complained that I woke him when I fed Lauren during the night. His concern was for himself only. Jason never rocked her or helped with her in any way, but he constantly criticized what I did: how I held her, how I calmed her down. He even hated the songs I sang to her. Nothing I did escaped his negative judgment.

I could drown out all his negative words with the happiness I felt just holding Lauren in my arms. If he had only limited himself to verbal abuse, I could have borne it. But no. That wasn't enough for Jason. Shortly after Lauren was born, Jason started attacking me while I held her. In his anger, he would pin me to the wall, push in my eyes, grab my head, and then push me to the floor, with Lauren in my arms the whole time. I feared so for Lauren; how could she be a normal child when she was witness to such abuse? Even before she was born, I had fears that she wouldn't be normal because of the abuse her father put me through while I was pregnant.

My mother stayed with us for one week after I returned home from the hospital, and she witnessed some of Jason's abuse. She was traumatized, but also confused. What could she do? How could she defend me from such an angry, irrational man? So she followed tradition and remained respectful and calm. She focused all her attention on Lauren as well as cooking and cleaning. We talked a little about the abuse, but I wasn't ready to reveal the full picture of my life with Jason. When my mother left, I know she was very sad and very worried.

Lauren's birth didn't change Jason one bit. He continued to lie all the time, to make up stories, and to believe them, no matter how ridiculous. He humiliated me regularly and attacked me--sometimes verbally, sometimes physically--if I said anything about his family. He would raise me up with a compliment or a kind word and then tear me down at his convenience depending on how competitive or insecure he was feeling. He always undercut me when I told him of some success I had in life or work, even though I complimented him on his achievements and always supported him in his choices and profession.

When Lauren was two months old, Jason and I were arguing about something his parents had said. I had Lauren in my arms, but I could not stop her screaming. I got away from Jason and locked myself in the bathroom. He promised to be quiet, so I came out. But, instead, he pushed me up against a wall and attacked my eyes again. He told me I had to stop arguing and screaming before he would let me go. He said, "You need to learn to stop talking, stop arguing." He did not free me until I was completely silent.

After he let me go, I went into our bedroom to comfort Lauren. Once I got over the fear that something bad would happen to Lauren, I became angry. Angry at Jason, angry at our life together, angry at myself for not doing anything about it. I asked myself, "Is there an escape from this?" I thought about calling the police, but I didn't know what they could do. I didn't know my rights. After a long time of rocking her and singing to her, Lauren fell asleep. Jason came into the room and acted as though nothing had happened; he just wanted to be normal. The anger, the pain, and the hurt were strong in me, but I managed to push them down. I determined I would try to do what Jason wanted so that Lauren could have a good life. At the time, I believed that a "good life" for Lauren was living in one home with both parents. I thought I could make myself the wife Jason wanted so that my child would be safe and comfortable and have the home I had dreamed of for her. I also wanted to live a life that was consistent with the values of my culture and religion, both of which strongly discouraged divorce.

Despite Jason's treatment of me, I tried to make a good home for us. Every night I cooked the best meals I could. I kept the house clean and organized, and his clothes were always clean and put away. He was never satisfied. When I organized his closet and papers, he would complain that I had confused things, and he didn't like what I had done. It was impossible to please him or to get him to see anything good in what I had done. In every positive situation, he saw something negative to nag and complain about. I never asked Jason to help me with the housework. Occasionally, he would vacuum the carpet and then tell people that he did the chores at home because I wouldn't do them. Although I tried to do everything expected of a wife, he chose to project this false image of me and he would give credibility to all his parents' doubts. Didn't he realize such lies also hurt his image?

Judgments and Insults

Jason often confused me with his contradictory words. Out of the blue, he would tell me I was a very smart woman, but then he would undercut that by saying that the type of engineering degree I had was not in real engineering. Another time, he told me my fingers and neck were too short, and then he told me how beautiful I was. He often told me how much he wanted me to be successful at work, but then he would interrupt my work by harassing me with messages and phone calls to complain about things that he didn't like. Before Jason started locking his computer, cellphone and everything else about his "other life", I had found pornography videos on his laptop; I was dumbfounded and saddened. When I confronted him with it, he claimed that the videos downloaded by themselves and he had no idea what it was; just like every other excuse I heard from Jason: "I don't know what you are talking about", "I have no idea where this came from", "you are crazy", and "you need help".

Any conversation we had always wound up being about him. If I said I had a headache, he would say, "I have two." If I complained at all about my work, he would cut me off and say, "Let me tell you about mine." Jason gave me about five seconds to talk before he started talking about himself. I never came home to a friend. I came home to a selfish, judgmental, and ruthless person who abused me verbally or physically according to his mood, and then told me he loved me, who provoked me and then criticized me for yelling, who insulted my family and then denied saying anything about them.

Jason's harassment during my work hours turned into outright cruelty. Several times, he threatened that he was going to take Lauren from daycare and take her away. Each time, I left my work in tears and drove at full speed to the daycare so he couldn't take her and hide her. When I got there, Lauren was safe inside, and Jason was nowhere to be seen. When I called him to ask where he was, he would laugh and ridicule me for believing him. I never could trust that he wouldn't take Lauren, so each time he called, it was the same routine. I was ever fearful of Lauren being alone with Jason because he constantly told me that I should beat her to discipline her; that is what his Bible said.

Jason often used the Bible to back up his positions, but he consistently twisted Biblical passages and scenes to make them conform to his ideas. For example, he said that when Jesus talked in the Temple, he raged and called the traders stupid. Of course, that's what Jason believed. And Jason constantly preached that the Bible insists that women must be submissive to their husbands. He told me that God wanted me to accept my destiny (Jason's abusing me?) without complaint. It was my cross to carry.

Using this same kind of emotional blackmail, Jason threatened to call my family and tell them we were getting a divorce if I didn't promise to treat him better, to do exactly as he told me to do. I gave into his demands many times because I didn't want any harm to come to my parents because of issues in my marriage. I knew Jason would not harm my parents physically, but I was well aware of the judgment against divorce in my culture. Damage would be done to my parents' reputation and their honor. People who judged them negatively because of my divorce would also cut them off socially. It would be a sad and isolating situation for my parents or so I thought.

Jason's stinginess became even more evident when we bought a house after Lauren was born. There are only two reasons that Jason would spend money on Lauren or me. First, he liked to make himself look good and play Father of the Year or Husband of the Year. Second, he would occasionally buy me something after he has been violent with me. Otherwise, I took care of all my expenses and Lauren's expenses. Although my salary was not very large at the new job I had found locally, I was able to furnish Lauren's room, and I bought all our kitchen necessities and all the house basics. I paid for my daughter's birthdays, for all our social commitments, for everything we needed that Jason didn't believe was necessary which is quite a lot. His contribution was paying the mortgage, and he reminded me every day that he provided a roof over my head. When we shopped together, he asked a thousand questions about each purchase and tried to justify not buying anything at all. I ended buying the house furnishings myself from my money so that we would have decent cups and plates to use for dinner guests. Of course, having these things made him look good, and he acted as though he's the one who provided everything. He wanted me to spend my money because he was always afraid that if I had any left, I would send it to my family. He insisted that all the money we earned must stay in our own family, even though I found out later that he sent money to his family in Jordan without telling me. He was full of doubt and always blaming me wrongfully.

SHAME AND HUMILIATION

It is difficult to recount all the shameful things that Jason did to my family, my friends, and me. Shortly after we moved to the Midwest, a dear friend planned to drive down from Chicago to congratulate us on our wedding. It's a six-hour drive. After she had been on the road for four hours, Jason and I had a fight. He told me to call my friend on her cell phone and tell her to turn around and go back. I was embarrassed to do that, and I thought Jason would get over his anger by the time she arrived. He didn't! He kicked my friend out of the house and told her to drive back to Chicago. She was frightened and in tears. That wasn't enough for him; he proceeded to regale her with lies about me and to tell her what a wicked person I was. I wanted to hide and never show my face again, but my friend was kind and understanding. She warned me, though, that Jason was unstable, and I needed to be careful.

Many times, Jason made me decline dinner invitations at the last minute. This happened so frequently that friends told me we had been disrespectful. If he didn't make me cancel, Jason would refuse to go until I begged him to get in the car and go, and we would invariably arrive late—sometimes hours late.

Jason would beat me up, and then bring me roses and expect me to keep quiet. He terrorized his daughter by screaming at her and shaking her, even though she was only one year old. But then he would tell her that he loved her—just like he did after hurting me. It was hard for me to see this and to see how Lauren ran away from her father. She didn't trust him and never wanted to go anywhere with him. Of course, I was scared to death to leave her in his care.

Often, while in the car, when Jason would get mad he would slam the dashboard and scream even louder at Lauren to shut her up; her and I would be terrified; and while he continued his act I would move to the back of the car and make silly faces and appease her fear so she would snap out of her tense feelings; I wanted her to believe his behavior was a funny act and she shouldn't be scared because I was laughing and asking her to do the same; it was so disturbing that I couldn't shied Lauren enough from his animosity.

My pride often kept me from fighting against Jason's abuse. Knowing that, he would use my pride against me to make me give up things he knew I wanted. He would try to get me to say I needed money, and that was the reason I needed him. So I would say no, I didn't want any more. He would ask why I was taking gifts to my family and call them "beggars" so I would not take things to them. He taunted me about my desire to have my name on our house's title, saying it meant I wanted a divorce and was after his money. I denied all of his accusations and justified not standing up to him by telling myself that we were married and loved each other. He frequently used this strategy to make me keep quiet and prevent me from going after what I was entitled to.

Jason's bad temper and tendency toward verbal abuse created difficulties for him at his work as well. The hospital administration reprimanded him for his disrespect and aggressiveness toward the nurses. When he received these warnings, he would treat the nurses with smiles and kindness in hopes that they would forget his earlier behavior.

Jason insisted on absolute control. In the winter, he seemed to want us to freeze. He wouldn't let me turn up the heater, so I had to wear four layers at home and more when I was sleeping. He didn't care what his child might be feeling. And in the summer, we suffocated because he wouldn't let us cool the house properly. Jason did this not only to control, but also because it was another way to save his money. His stinginess was greater than his concern for his wife and child.

One day, I found out that Jason had more e-mail accounts than I thought. When I confronted him, he said I was delusional. He called me sick and crazy and told me I needed a psychiatrist. After telling me he couldn't live with me anymore, he sent me e-mails with information about psychiatrists.

I shared things about my family with Jason in hopes of getting close to him. I told him that one of my sisters had broken her engagement. Jason's response was, "This poor guy never had a chance in your family just like I didn't." He had no sympathy for my sister; he wanted only to have sympathy for himself and make my family look bad. When another of my sisters was coping with depression, Jason heard about it from someone he knew in Lebanon. His response to her situation was to say to me, "Craziness runs in your family." He turned my sister's illness against my family and me.

Jason's Parents Visit

During the spring two years after our marriage, I learned two days ahead of their visit that Jason's parents were coming to visit for eleven days. The only part of that visit that was pleasant was the dinner we had in St. Louis after we picked them up at the airport. The minute we were in our own home, the circus began.

Jason's mother imitated me in my style of gift giving. She opened her suitcase and dramatically presented gifts to Jason, Lauren, and me. As it was my style not hers, the performance seemed sad and artificial.

Just like her son, Jason's mother was constantly critical. She complained that my dishes were too heavy, and there was always too much food. She asked why Jason wasn't phoning his sister as often as he used to, implying that it was my fault. We took them to dinners at expensive restaurants, but Jason's mother complained, "You're making us fat." The worst part was her nagging about Lauren. She criticized the way I washed and fed my daughter—as if I hadn't been doing it right since Lauren was born.

In a strange twist, Jason's mother tried to act like my ally. She told me that in the first year of their marriage, Jason's dad had told his parents every little thing that happened in their lives. It had bothered her a lot, but they had come to an understanding, and then it was better. When she heard Jason yell at me, she'd tell him to work on his anger; he was too much like his father;

Unfortunately, my mother-in-law's attempts to be friendly were cancelled out by her other actions. During the day, she, her husband, and Jason would go into the guest bedroom to talk for hours and leave me alone with Lauren. One day, I overheard them talking about my income, what I spent it on, and the amount of money in our 401(k). When I confronted Jason about telling his parents about our private finances, he said I was delusional; they weren't talking about that at all. The general atmosphere of secretiveness and my exclusion made me distrustful.

While his parents were with us, I bought many gifts for Jason's mother, and I let her take many items from my own closet. I was happy to try to make her happy, but that didn't happen. Instead of thanking me, his mother suggested that I gave gifts to feed my ego. She said, "So, you love giving your stuff to people?" I received no credit for anything I did. Jason accused me of being superficial and materialistic. He said I was trying to buy his parents' love with gifts and implied that they agreed with this.

The final blow came on the day they left. Jason's father handed me five hundred dollars. In my culture, it is typical for any gift be given at the beginning of a visit, and for the hosts to express gratitude with excitement and graciousness. Handing me money at the end of their visit was a violation of cultural etiquette. I felt so ashamed and humiliated. This crass gift made it seem like he was paying for a stay in a hotel. I had opened my home and tried to open my heart to these people. How could he do such an insulting, demeaning thing as give me money, as though I expected payment for my hospitality? I wondered if they had added up the amounts we had spent for lunches and dinners to arrive at the amount of five hundred dollars.

After this visit, I started standing up for myself even more. I had gotten nowhere with Jason by being nice to his family, so I would try to fight against his insults and commands. But I was also sorry for Jason. He had been manipulated and controlled and may never be happy. I came to think of him as a sad, depressed person.

LAUREN'S BAPTISM

In the late summer after my in-laws visited, I decided to baptize Lauren. Of course, there would be a conflict over this because Jason had deceived me about his religion. He and his family didn't believe in baptizing a child at a young age, if at all. We argued about it and I told him that I married him believing that he was Christian Orthodox not Church of Christ or Jehovah's Witness. I held my ground until Jason finally gave in and I left with Lauren for Lebanon, where my parents and I planned the baptism. In the Lebanese culture, parents enthusiastically and generously celebrate important events in their children's lives, and I intended to give Lauren the most glorious celebration that I could. Jason gave me a budget of two thousand dollars for the event. It would have been almost impossible to feed about fifty people for that amount of money and to pay for cake, decorations, and other incidentals. As such, my dad decided to pay the difference.

When Jason learned what a large celebration I was planning, he frequently phoned and texted to call me superficial and greedy. He hated spending money even when it was my father's or mine. Two days before the baptism, Jason came to Lebanon as planned. He told me that his relatives weren't going to attend the baptism.

That made choosing godparents difficult. I had chosen one of my sisters as godmother, but no one would be there to represent Jason's side of the family even though I had invited all of them. I was still struggling with whom to choose as godfather when his parents made a last-minute decision to come. I was happy to name Jason's dad as the godfather. My mother-in-law, though, had to criticize me even for that. She made sure to tell me that I hadn't done anything special; it is the norm to name one godparent from each side of the family.

The baptism was beautiful and the celebration was joyful. My family and friends showered Lauren with gold, money, and other precious gifts. I laid all the gifts on the cake table for everyone to see. It was a wonderful sight, but Jason's parents insisted on spoiling things once again. They pulled me aside and told me to hide the gifts so no one would steal them. I was horrified and embarrassed to think they could suspect any of my family or friends or even the restaurant staff of being thieves. I refused to put the gifts away. Then they sent the same message with Jason, and he came to make me do it. I knew he would make a scene if I didn't do as he told me to, so I put the gifts away.

After all the festivities concluded, it was time to pay the two-thousand-dollar bill for the restaurant. What a humiliating moment. As our guests watched, Jason loudly evaluated every waiter, every service provided, and every bit of food. He then began trying to negotiate the price. The owner felt trapped. He called me over and reminded me that we had already agreed on the price. I told Jason just to pay the money. He wouldn't pay until he received a discount of two hundred dollars. I was crushed with shame. My father and I had given our word on the original price and felt that Jason had cheated the owner. Because Jason made an ostentatious display of counting out the money, everyone noticed, and my dad asked me if I needed more money. I said no, and our party left the restaurant. I am still ashamed when I remember this event, and I hope never to meet that owner again.

That was not the end of the rudeness and insult that Jason and his family showed while they were in Lebanon. My family invited Jason's parents to sleep over for the two days they were in Lebanon, but they refused. My family invited them to dinner to welcome them, but they refused. They stayed with one of Jason's aunts in Beirut. Jason and I went to greet them there and were stunned at their coldness not only toward me, but also toward Jason's aunt. His parents behaved as though they had come to Lebanon against their will and as though I was responsible for that burden. They even complained to Jason's aunt that we had invited them at the last minute, which is why they hadn't had time to arrange a rental car and needed their sister to drive them to Lauren's baptism. The reality is quite different. Despite the fact that Jason's mother hates her sister-in-law, she would rather stay with relatives than pay to stay at a hotel and rent a car.

Even as a guest, Jason's mother wouldn't avoid being hurtful. She stated loudly and clearly that she hated Lebanon and hated being in Lebanon. How could she be so callous when she was a guest in a Lebanese home—and the home of a relative? How mortifying for her sister-in-law and husband, who are Lebanese. I found out later that my mother-in-law's need to control was at the heart of this conflict. Early in their marriage, my father-in-law sent money to his sister, who at that time was in need of financial support. Gradually, my mother-in-law stopped him from doing this and kept him away from contact with his other family members. She did to her husband what Jason tried so hard to do to me.

While in Lebanon just before Lauren's baptism I wanted to make sure we can issue a Lebanese passport for Lauren. Jason and I borrowed my sister's car and headed to Beirut. We decided that I would drive the two hours before we went to greet his family at his aunt's home. The drive was a horror movie when Jason decided to lash out his feelings being in Lebanon and trashing my family. It escalated to him hitting me and beating on the car's dashboard like a maniac while I was driving; Beirut's traffic was bumper to bumper and we sure gave the audience a show. I was scared and embarrassed and the yelling got worst by the minute; as he was pushing me and terrifying me, I got so disoriented which landed the car on a divider breaking down the car. Lucky enough we were very close to a car repair shop where we changed the tires and continued the journey; the car's damage as I knew of it a year later was terrible and I made it seem like it was just an accident in my story to my family. While we waited for the passport to be issued we sat at a McDonald where he left me sitting there broken and confused; I had no idea where he decided to go for a walk. I followed him begging him to calm down; and on the streets of Beirut, Jason's anger continued where he chastised me screaming so loud and making embarrassing hand gestures that everyone passing by looked shamefully at the abusive scene. We collected the passport and headed to meet his family pretending to be at peace; how much longer can I mask my sadness and the intolerable relationship with Jason?

Unwelcome in My Husband's Family

My mother-in-law never loved me, while she continued to tell her son that she did. One can feel love, and it is obvious she had none for me. I got in the way between her and her son. She needed her son to stay the little boy she could control. She didn't want him to leave her and have a life of his own. Throughout my pregnancy, she never called to check how I felt. I think she didn't want to make me feel important for being pregnant. Showing any regard for me when I was not feeling well would have put me in the limelight. She couldn't have anyone feeling better or worse than she did. Like a three-year-old, she had to be the center of attention.

I confided to Jason that I thought his mother never loved me because I am Lebanese and that she would have preferred him to marry a Palestinian woman like her. Sometime later, Jason turned this around and told his mother that I hated her because she was a Palestinian. With this lie, Jason gave his mother the opportunity to stop even pretending that she liked me.

Jason whispered all his troubles in his mother's ear, and she manipulated him emotionally. She even has told him to lie to me and to keep secrets from me. I never knew anything about the activities of Jason's family, yet he talked to them all day long, and they knew everything I did and said. For example, Jason's sister was four months pregnant before I heard about it. And then, I heard about it from my aunt in Lebanon. I didn't know if his brother got into college or what was he studying. Jason's parents had immigrated to Canada, and I didn't know until after they were there. Most of the things I knew about Jason' family I learned from some random connection. I didn't want to pry, but it made me depressed to know that Jason's loyalty resided with his family. I began to feel he wanted a wife only for sex and for his public image.

Jason consistently refused my requests unless he knew his family would approve what I asked. For example, I suggested that we go to Mexico for a vacation. Jason said it was dangerous and corrupt there. He told me we would be murdered or at least have our belongings stolen. But then he spoke to one of his aunts who said they had had a wonderful time in Mexico. Then, suddenly, he thought Mexico was a great place, and we should plan a trip, as though it had been completely his idea. I honestly think that if his family said hell was OK, then hell would be OK and we could go. If his family said buying this or doing that or flying there was OK, then it would be OK with Jason. But if I suggested something to do or somewhere to go, Jason gave one hundred reasons why it was a bad idea. I truly believe Jason has been brainwashed and manipulated, and he has tried to do the same to me.

My in-laws judged me negatively because I dressed nicely and always tried to look my best. They told Jason that I couldn't be religious if I cared so much about appearances. I'm glad I was strong enough to tell them that dressing nice and hosting nice dinners has nothing to do with faith, and these actions do not categorize me as materialistic. The sad part, though, is that Jason believed what his parents said. He would tell me that I was a devil or an atheist. They quoted the Bible to him in support of their views of me, and he swallowed every word. He would try to convince me they were right. When I didn't agree, Jason would yell at me as though he truly hated me.

Jason's parents never once taught him how to be a gentleman, instead they encouraged his behaviors of crushing me and making me more and more submissive. They enjoyed him putting me in place especially his mother; his relationship with his mother made me sick and almost felt incestual where she used him day in and day out for her self-assurance and selfish motives; almost like Maleficent needing the mirror to tell her she is beautiful. She never truly let go, my husband was never present in our marriage.

DECEPTION

When Lauren was six months old, Jason took us to Arizona, supposedly to get away and have a good time. What was to be a vacation for us turned out to be nothing but business. With his relatives' help, Jason had bought a house in Arizona as an investment property. Our whole time there was taken up with evaluating the property. Earlier that year, Jason had brought me papers to sign, but wouldn't let me read them. He told me they were nothing important. When the divorce process began, I found out that I had signed away all my rights to the property. Much later, I would find out much more about how Jason hurt me financially. He was always so secretive about money that I had no idea that he had been sending large sums to his parents, thus taking away what was legitimately Lauren's and mine.

While in Arizona, we stayed with Jason's aunt and uncle, who got to meet Lauren for the first time. This made Jason's mother jealous and angry because this trip was before Jason's parents first visit and my mother-in-law hadn't met her yet. She was angry that her sister got to see Lauren first. So she arranged a trip to see us as quickly as possible. She and my father-in-law arrived one month after we came back from Arizona. Jason's mother likes to be the first in everything. In fact, many people who knew her told me that she was very competitive and a very jealous person.

When Lauren was a year and a half old, Jason treated her and me to a trip to Las Vegas. Since Las Vegas was the first place that we had been happy together, we thought this trip would rekindle our love. What a mistake. Everywhere we walked and whatever we talked about resulted in some complaint from Jason. Worse than Jason's treatment, though, was the involvement of his family. His parents were angry that I agreed to go to Las Vegas, but I hadn't yet gone to visit them in Canada. Even though Jason had not been to visit with them in Canada, they focused on me. They told Jason this and when he told me, he was in a rage even though this trip had been his idea. He scorned me again and said I had a "black heart."

Perhaps the most unsettling thing that happened in Vegas was one that gave me a glimpse into the future. Jason showed me that his hand was bruised from carrying the stroller, and I felt very sorry that he was hurting. The next day, I saw that he had taken a picture of the bruise. Quickly, I made the connection. I had threatened to show the bruises he gave me to the police. Even though the idea was absurd, I was sure that Jason intended to use this photograph to accuse me of bruising him if I ever told anyone about my bruises.

I came to the conclusion that only a deranged person would go to such lengths to protect his world of lies and denial. We were on vacation! Seeing the sights and watching Lauren's enjoyment was my focus; Jason had his mind on other things. He was obviously calculating how he could get the better of me should a divorce and custody battle become a reality. Once again, the hope to make a fresh start in our marriage wound up in the trash.

Jason's mother continued her hypocritical ways. One of Jason's sisters had just moved with her husband close to her parents in Canada. Even though Jason and I had been married for three years, this was the first time that his family recognized my birthday. His mother called me multiple times to wish me a happy birthday. She and one of his sisters baked a cake and took pictures of the cake with lit candles; they sent e-mails and texts saying they wanted to sing happy birthday to me over the phone. Their gesture was confusing to me; Jason's mother had never done anything that kind for me. But her intent became clear to me after a while. Jason's parents had a new son-in-law; this was all an act meant to give a lesson to him and his family. My mother-in-law was telling him, "Your parents will need to treat our daughter very well. Look how we treat and love our daughter-in-law." It was a farce, but very well played.

GOING TO JORDAN AGAIN

A couple of months later, Lauren, Jason, and I went to Jordan for the wedding of one of Jason's cousins. I was excited to go because it would be Lauren's first trip to the region, and I really enjoyed Jason's extended family. Jason and I agreed to stay at a hotel because I told him I would be more comfortable there. My mother-in-law disliked this and badgered Jason to stay at his sister's house instead. She called me and told me his sister had prepared a room, and it was not nice of me to keep Jason away from his family. She insisted, "Let him see his family and only sleep in the hotel late at night," suggesting that I intended not to let Jason see his family at all. We agreed to spend the days at his sister's house, and indeed, per his mom's direction, his sister made sure we were with the family for the whole day, never getting to the hotel until midnight. Through it all, Jason acted as though his sister was more important than me, always paying attention to her wishes and those of his mother. Who was I to have a say in this? He let his family control him and control us, and he didn't defend me or protect me. I felt that I was one against them. They never tried to understand me or appreciate me. Instead, they alienated me from them and tried to alienate Jason from me.

I didn't want to stay with his sister because Jason always embarrassed me in front of his family, and I was still traumatized from the last trip. One day, when we had a short time away from his family, I told Jason that I felt more comfortable being in a hotel, and if he loved me, he would care about my comfort. His response was typical: screaming and yelling and pushing me about. Then, he started spitting at me repeatedly and saying that I was wrong not to want to stay at his sister's house. Lauren was in my arms, telling him, "Stop, Daddy. That's not nice." I was boiling in anger, so I spat back at him once. Of course, he ran to his parents with the story that I had spat on him.

It was the first time that I did to him what he had done to me. All the times he hit me I never retaliated because I knew what a coward he was. He would reverse the story and say that I had lied. I had let myself be humiliated and abused and hit and attacked without retaliation not only because I was scared of him, but also, at the end of the day, I wanted to have done the right thing. But this time, I had retaliated. Never in a million years would I think I could have done that, and I was truly ashamed. I resolved to avoid confrontation with Jason whenever I could. Even though Jason and his family would accuse me of acting badly toward them all, I wanted to know in my heart that I had nothing worthy of blame. When Lauren, a two-year-old, screamed at him and said, "Don't hit Mommy," I began to understand how important it was that I not take Jason's physical and emotional abuse any longer.

It would take time, though, before Jason's behavior and an opportunity for action on my part came together. I had been an abused wife for over three years. Jason had me under control to the point that I didn't believe I could do without him. He had made me a very much weaker version of myself—the version he wanted me to be.

In spite of the way Jason acted around Lauren, he kept saying he wanted more children. I told him that ours was a toxic relationship, and it was unfair for us to have another child until we could resolve our issues. I feared for Lauren's welfare around such a volatile father. I love children and always wanted a big family like the one I came from. But I am also a mother who wants healthy, stable, and happy kids. And thank God that I was able to shelter Lauren from the worst of her father's abuse so that she is now a happy child. That's where my focus had to be now.

LEBANON

From Jordan, we went to Lebanon. Jason stayed with us there for four days; Lauren and I stayed for another two weeks. When he needed to return to the United States, Jason not only forced me to take Lauren with us to the airport, but he made a horrible scene when we arrived there. He insisted that we all get out of the car to say good-bye to him. The airport is dangerous, and I refused to have my parents and Lauren leave the safety of the car. I got out of the car in an attempt to please him, but that wasn't enough for Jason. He hadn't managed to control everyone as he wanted to, so he left in a bitterly angry mood.

I could no longer keep my unhappiness from my parents, and I told them all the misery that had been my life with Jason. By this time, my mother had seen some of Jason's cruelty, and my sisters knew some minimal details, but now I told everything to my parents. I was ashamed, humiliated, and deeply depressed, but I believed I had to tell them. Of course, they were horrified, though my father seemed to have some inkling of the kind of man Jason was. We cried together, prayed together, and talked into the night.

In the end, we all decided I should try again. Be more patient. See how much he missed me after our two weeks' separation. We agreed on this even though Jason and I were constantly having fights via texts and e-mails during these two weeks. My parents and I believe in the commitment of marriage, and we believed there must be a way to work things out. I made up my mind to go back home and work as hard as I could to make my marriage to Jason a successful one. I knew I had the strong support of my parents and my sisters in this endeavor, and I had faith that a good life was still possible. In Lebanon during those two weeks, I had found a bit of myself that I had lost in my life with Jason; some of my self-confidence returned.

How could I have anticipated the difficulty of the trip back? My parents dropped Lauren and me off. They encouraged me to be confident and happy, and I felt so at that moment. And I felt strong—strong enough to fight for the life I wanted. I was ready to return home and begin.

After entering the airport, I immediately began to feel ill. I had pain in my chest, I was dizzy, I couldn't see clearly, and I was shivering. I thought I was dying and could worry only about what would happen to Lauren. I managed to get a wheel chair and received assistance getting to the security check. There, they checked my luggage while I was barely able to stand. I really don't remember how I managed to get on the plane. The flight attendants tried to help by giving me water and tea, but my symptoms did not abate. I became convinced that I was sick from fear of returning to my life with Jason.

The plane descended for a nine-hour layover in Jordan. I called Jason and told him about my illness. He said I was having a panic attack and needed medicine. There was a pharmacy at the airport, and I went there to ask for medicine. I was on the line with Jason while I was talking to the pharmacist, and Jason accused me of flirting with him. Even while I was begging him for help, he was accusing me of doing wrong. Because the pharmacist couldn't give me medicine under the circumstances, Jason said he could do no more. That was his cold, matter-of-fact advice, which he gave with no apparent concern. I might have been any of his faceless patients.

In my panic and pain, my thoughts were almost completely with Lauren—what she was going through and what might happen to her. All of a sudden I remembered how Jason had frightened me any time I went out of the United States with Lauren. He told me he would notify the government in Lebanon or Jordan that I had kidnapped Lauren, and they would take her away from me. Remembering that cruel threat made my fear and panic almost uncontrollable.

What came next was deeply cutting and cruel—cruel even for Jason. He said, "God is punishing you for what you're doing to me." Jason had an image of what I should be, and I did not measure up to that image. To him, I was a bad person with a dark heart. I was not righteous in the way the Bible told him I should be. So he believed I was acting in a way that would lead to my being punished. He went on to tell me I was a disgrace to his family, and I should go back to Lebanon because we were going to get a divorce. I felt destroyed. The shaking and chest pains started up again. I began vomiting uncontrollably. Then, he said he wasn't coming to pick us up in Chicago the next day. By that time, I just didn't care; I was too sick and worried about how I would care for Lauren.

The thirteen-hour flight to Chicago took the last of my waning strength. I had to get a wheel chair to get through the airport. All through the flight, my whole body twitched and shook—my knees, my arms, my face, even my teeth. Lauren needed attention, but I was barely able to care for her. Some Advil and some of Lauren's Benadryl were all I had to help me stay alert through the flight.

You will be shocked at what I tell you next, but it is the truth. When we landed in Chicago, Jason was there to greet us despite his threats of divorce. When I saw him, I ran to him and gave him a tight hug. I was so happy to see his familiar face that all the animosity and anger I had felt melted away. Jason even seemed happy to see me. We talked about the panic attack and what could be done about it. There was no anger or shouting as we returned home. My resolve to make our marriage work came back in that instant.

Change of Plans

When Lauren was almost two years old, we bought another home in the small Illinois town Jason worked in even though we had agreed to stay for only three years. Before we came to the Midwest, I was well on my way in my career. I had hoped we would move to a place where I could advance it again. But Jason wanted to sign a contract for another three years because he felt he could earn more money in his present job than he could elsewhere. Jason argued that he might be unhappy in any of the places he could get a new position, so I agreed to stay because I didn't want him to be unhappy. I didn't want Jason to feel insecure because he wasn't making the money he wanted to make, and I told myself that this extra money would help make Lauren's future more secure.

After we moved to our new home, my mother and one of my sisters came to visit. My sister stayed only one week, and we drove her to Ohio for a medical internship. It was a nine-hour drive that I'll never forget. Jason kept up his shouting and insulting us all and slamming on the dashboard throughout the trip. Lauren was in the back crying. My mother and sister tried to reason with Jason, but neither could make him stop his behavior. I felt like I was having another panic attack, and I begged him to stop the car. When he did, my sister and I went into a gas station, and she stayed with me until I was calm enough to get back in the car. My mother had been able to get Lauren settled and we continued the trip.

We got my sister settled in the dorm, and my mom came back with us to stay for another week. It happened to be one of Jason's weeks off from work. It was impossible to tell that he was the same man who had screamed at us during the drive to Ohio. He was kind and attentive to my mother. While I was at work, they went for walks, and Jason texted me that she even laughed at his jokes. In that week, I really thought Jason could change.

That feeling didn't last long. My mother had returned to Lebanon, and my sister returned to visit for another four days. One day when I was at work, she called me and told me I had to come and handle the situation. She was overwhelmed because Jason was yelling at her and trying to make her defend herself for something she didn't understand. He belittled her and told her she would never be as good a physician as he was. No matter what she said, he wouldn't let the matter drop.

I learned all this by talking with my sister on the phone as I drove home from work. I was able to quiet my sister and get her to go to bed. Then I tried to talk with Jason; he merely patronized me. He told me that he loved me and that I must learn to control myself. I was torn between loyalty to my sister and my loyalty to Jason. I wanted him to believe that I was a good wife and wouldn't put my family before him and Lauren. So I dropped the discussion and hoped we would be able to figure it all out at a later time.

The next day, Jason didn't want me to take my sister to the airport; he thought I wanted to be alone with her so I could tell her things about him. Even though he had come off the night shift, he insisted on driving us so he could monitor our conversation. Later, I overheard him tell his mother how tired he was and that I had made him drive my sister to the airport.

Attempts to Heal

That fall, Jason and I started in earnest to work on our relationship. We talked—sometimes without arguing—and it seemed we might compromise. But mostly Jason stated what he wanted me to do and what he wanted me to give up. I had given up so much of my life style and most of my friends already. I didn't see what else I could do. We usually reached a stalemate.

The panic attacks persisted. It took several visits to the emergency room over the course of a month and care from my doctor to get them under control. During that time, I suffered great cruelty from Jason. When I was having an attack, he would say that sex would calm me down and force himself on me. When I tried to refuse to have sex with him, he threatened to sleep with other women. He continually told me I needed to see a psychiatrist because I was going crazy. I suspect he believed that if I did see a psychiatrist, he would be able to take Lauren from me.

After the three months and with help from my doctor, I had no more panic attacks, but I began to have frequent anxiety attacks, especially during arguments with Jason. He seemed to delight in forcing these arguments to see me crumble into anxiety. He loved to see me weak and mocked me when I had an attack.

Jason began leaving the house in the morning and not returning until after midnight. He refused to tell me where he had been. This was something

I just could not live with, especially knowing how he would treat me if I ever did the same thing.

During this time, my mother and sister came to visit. My sister was doing another medical internship with a pediatrician in our area. Even though they were guests and family, Jason treated them poorly. He shouted at my mother and upset her terribly. He complained constantly and forced his opinions and criticisms about our lifestyle into every conversation. He refused to listen to any of us when we asked him to stop shouting; he hardly gave us a chance to talk. He did this again and again with my mom and my sister. He humiliated them with his behavior and criticism.

During this visit, my sister would care for Lauren so that Jason and I could go out and work on healing our relationship. Despite all she had seen of our relationship and Jason's behavior, she continued to talk me into trying to reconcile with him. Somehow she—and even I—wanted to believe that heart-to-heart talks could heal the wounds and bring Jason and me together again. I wanted badly for her to be right and agreed to try as hard as I could. I told Jason this, but I also told him that our working together had to produce change. If it did not, it would be my last attempt.

One night another couple picked us up to go out to a party with them. Jason seemed to enjoy himself. He went out of his way to treat me well. When they brought us home, Jason asked them to come in. Although he was gracious at first, it wasn't long before he reverted to his nasty personality. He bossed the woman around and contradicted her when she spoke. The next day, my colleague got in touch with me. He said he didn't think Jason was mentally stable. He remarked that Jason treated people well at the party, but when he got back into his comfort zone, he was once again arrogant and disrespectful. My emotions about this were mixed. I was pained to know that other people were aware of Jason's unacceptable behavior. At the same time, I felt sorry for him. What would happen to his reputation as word of this behavior got around?

On one of the nights that my sister babysat for us, I gave Jason an ultimatum. I told him people felt sorry for me because of what he did and how he discounted all I had to say. I was tired of shutting up in public so that people wouldn't notice our arguing. I begged him to help me understand his behavior and why he was so inconsistent. Finally, I told him, "I love you, but I'm not having this conversation again. Next time, I'll divorce you." Jason threatened to divorce me ever since we got married; he told me day in and day out about all the options he had being with other women and how much he didn't want me; his goals were to get me back in line, his line, through threats, indifference, disappearance, silent treatments and accusations of me being unfaithful; He was guilty of everything he accused me of; that's what narcissists do. Jason was very good at the Idolize phase, he can mimic the appropriate emotions of normal people to get the desired result or something that he needs; the farce was over very soon because Jason was incapable of love or emotional connections. Once I fell his prey again in this emotional roller coaster then the cycle of "I can take you or leave you" begins again. Not long after the idolize phase launches that Jason begins his web of lies and this is where he kept me in a confused state, looking for answers and most importantly, my sanity. His lies are so simple and subtle that I didn't even question them and when I did I was in for a storm of anger and gaslighting; He withheld information, pretended not to understand me by diverting the conversations, trivializing, forgetting and denying; I heard repeatedly: "is this another crazy idea you got from your family?", "I don't know what you are talking about?", "Are you really going to get angry over this little thing?", "I don't remember saying that", "you are imagining things that never happened"; he psychologically and emotionally abused me by making me question my sanity, my existence while he got away with lies challenging my memory and my emotional state every day. He was quick to accuse me of not trusting him, of being a jealous wife, of being a nag, and of making a big deal out of nothing. Living with Jason was an emotional suicide. Throughout our marriage, Jason believed that his presence is enough to foster and maintain trust, loyalty, affection and respect but he always managed down my expectations, *Just enough – Just In Time*, which allowed him to get away with more and more.

I expected Jason to argue, to protest, or to make excuses. He didn't. Instead, he insisted that he didn't want a divorce. He told me over and over that he loved me, that I was his "princess." By this time, I had heard those words too often to believe them. They were empty words that couldn't erase the yelling, the insults, the hitting, and all the other ways Jason had of showing that love was not what he felt for me.

My mother and sister saw the anxiety attacks I was having and were very worried. My sister said I should see a lawyer. Jason promised he wouldn't hurt me or yell at me anymore, however, so I didn't do as my sister suggested. I can see how weak—even crazy—this was now. I had been a victim of Jason's manipulation for several years. Responding differently than he had taught me to was frightening. At that moment, I did not have the courage, so I let myself be his victim one more time.

After they left, another of my sisters came to the United States to take the licensing exam for pharmacists and stayed with us for two weeks over Christmas and New Year's. Jason wanted my sister to think he was changing, so he bought special gifts for her and for me for Christmas. This gesture had a positive effect. Quick to forget Jason's abuse, I again believed that I saw change in him. He had never bought any of my sisters anything before. And he didn't yell at her. I hoped this meant a new beginning for us all.

On New Year's Eve, Jason worked the night shift at his hospital. I went out with Lauren and my sister to a friend's for the evening, but I began to miss Jason. My sister and I decided to take Lauren to the hospital so that Jason could spend a little of the holiday with her. Even though we waited in the parking lot until he was on break, Jason was not happy to see us and said it was wrong for us to come there. His coldness not only to my sister and me, but most importantly to his own daughter, was heartbreaking for me.

After the New Year, Jason, Lauren, my sister and I went with another couple to Nashville for three days, and I believed Jason had really started to change. I was happy to be with him in a long trip, and I believed we were living a new beginning. He was pleasant to everyone and quite courteous. That lasted for a day. Suddenly, he got into a loud argument with my sister and yelled at her in public. Then he started criticizing me and even yelling at me in front of the couple we were travelling with. I began to believe it wasn't possible for Jason to act in any other way toward me and possibly not toward my family.

When we got home from Nashville, Jason fought with my sister again and accused her of going through his things because I had asked her to help me tidy up and unpack. She had graciously agreed, but all Jason could see was negative intentions on my sister's part, the wish to pry into his personal business. Even though I asked her to help, Jason made accusations so demeaning and insulting that both my sister and I felt both angry and ashamed at the same time.

My sister had had it with Jason and the life he had created for Lauren and me. He was out of control in his screaming and attacking me in front of Lauren, who was terrified when these things happened. My sister asked Jason to leave the house. Of course, he said he wouldn't do that and stayed around and made more accusations. He phoned his parents and told them that my sister and I were against him and determined to exclude him. Finally, he just went to his room to be away from us. Before he did that, I found some courage. I looked him straight in the eye and said, "We're done! I'm going to divorce you" he responded saying "Are you sure?" and I said "Yes for sure".

After he left the room, my sister said if I stayed in that home with Jason any longer, they would have to put me in a mental institution. She told me to pack a bag: "Just what you need for you and Lauren." She figured that if we left, he would quickly realize what he'd lost and come to his senses. I knew better, but I didn't argue with her. I had finally accepted that Jason's actions would not change. Because of that, Lauren would always be in danger of abuse. I had allowed myself to be abused, but I would not let the same thing happen to Lauren.

Even understanding the reasons Jason had such control of me, before I left the house, I gave it a complete cleaning. I even did the laundry and changed the bed linen. Somehow, I couldn't escape from the need for Jason to see me as a good wife, even as I proceeded with divorcing him; I wanted to make sure he had all he needed by the time I come back: after he realizes what he is losing; I didn't know I wouldn't come back and that he would never appreciate what he had.

The only place I had to go was to the owner of Lauren's day care, who was a friend. She took care of Lauren, and I went with my sister to my lawyer. I told him I'd sign the divorce papers. I asked for the papers to be served to

Jason on a Saturday when he was home because I did not want him embarrassed at his work. Unfortunately, after several attempts to find him at home, he finally was served with the papers at his work, where he began shouting insults about me. Even though I had told him I was going to divorce him, he told people at his work that my leaving was a shock; he claimed he didn't understand it at all.

I was very frightened, and I needed my family. My mother booked the first flight from Lebanon that she could, so I dropped my sister off at the airport for her flight and stayed there overnight to wait for my mother's arrival. When she arrived, we sought shelter with my friend who owned the day care. She let us stay for a whole month.

I got texts from Jason every day. He wanted us to get back together but also told me what a bad person I was. I had anxiety attacks every day. I was, of course concerned for Lauren and myself, but I couldn't stop thinking about how Jason was doing, how he was feeling. My sympathy for him never left me in spite of his continued mistreatment of me.

TIME OF TURMOIL

It was calm and safe at my friend's home, who I felt was my only friend in the area at that time. It was essential for Lauren to have this calm, safe environment, and I badly needed a place where I could feel secure. By this time, I was overwhelmingly frightened of Jason.

My lawyer tried to get an order of protection for us, but there was a delay. My mother cared for Lauren during the day. She couldn't go to day care because I feared that Jason would come and take her from there. My lawyer told me to keep Lauren with me, so I was with her all the time after my work. My mother cooked and cleaned for our gracious hosts, and we had some quiet days. But in all of this, I couldn't stop feeling the horror of my situation: on my own with no savings, no home, and a very young daughter.

The turmoil with Jason never ended. He constantly sent texts to me, which I didn't answer because my lawyer told me not to do that. The texts, like most of my life with Jason, were confusing. In one, he begged me to give our marriage another chance. He said we had made a mistake in coming to this area; it wasn't right for us. He would resign and seek work elsewhere. And he suggested we try counseling. In other words, he offered many of the changes I had asked for. But in the next text, he would send a diatribe. He asked why I "blew out the candle of our marriage," and once again, he called me a wicked person.

One morning, Jason came to my work and brought me flowers. He included a card that read, "Will you marry me again?" I asked him why he'd want to marry the person he said such despicable things about, but he didn't have an answer. I told him to get out of my affairs; I couldn't face going through life with him. There was nothing genuine about his gesture. I saw it as just one more in the long string of his saying things or giving me gifts to make me forget the cruel treatment that came before.

Shortly after Lauren and I left our home, Jason's parents came and stayed with him at that home. Jason had phoned them with the news that I had left and taken Lauren, so they came to do what they could for him. Very soon after they arrived, they called my grandmother in New Jersey and told her how horrible I was and that I had taken Lauren away from Jason. Then they told her what a bad person I was and dredged up all kinds of lies about me, like that I had stolen Jason's money and taken all of our jewelry.

My grandmother was appalled. She had kept in touch with Jason's parents after the wedding, and they had always said good things about our marriage. The shock and confusion of this call made her ill. Thankfully, one of my cousins was with my grandmother and got her off that phone. My cousin phoned me, and I phoned my dad. He called Jason's parents and got a very hostile reception. My dad tried to defend me and said he had given Jason a wonderful woman who was well educated and had received honors degrees. My mother-in-law's response was, "You can shove her." After that, we all gave up on talking to Jason's parents. They would believe what they wanted to believe. They would defend themselves and their son in hateful ways, but we would not engage in that kind of behavior.

Contrary to what Jason's parents told my grandmother and many others, they took back the jewelry they had given to me at the wedding along with several gold pieces that Jason had given to me over the years of our marriage. Worse, they told everyone who would listen that I had stolen all the jewelry. I have come to believe that Jason and his parents have no shame, no decency, and no values. They are people who love to preach the Bible to others and who used religion to manipulate me into being submissive.

Jason and I and our lawyers had a private meeting in the courthouse in which Jason asked to be able to have Lauren for a five-day visit right away while his parents were still with him. When both my lawyer and I refused that request, Jason blew up and began yelling right there at his lawyer. In court, the judge granted him a three-day visit. Even though this was a one-time arrangement, I was sick about it. I did not want Lauren to be away from me because I was so fearful of her being with her father and grandparents. But I had no choice except to follow what the judge said. We arranged to meet at the day care, so I drove Lauren there and waited. Jason and his parents came, but when they saw my car, they kept driving. They waited for me to leave Lauren before they would get out of the car. How sad I was to have Lauren go with them. I knew they would try to poison her little mind against me. They can feel good about themselves only when they make someone else—usually me—look bad.

A few days before Jason's parents left, I went to the house to get some clothes for Lauren and me. Jason's mother watched me the whole time, but I didn't care. I was disgusted with all of them and ignored them as much as I could. When I was leaving, though, Jason helped take some of the things to my car. For a moment, I felt connected to him again. The old feelings of love and affection came back. And Jason must have felt some of the same. He said I should come back to the house with Lauren; he'd rent a place for himself. We agreed on that arrangement, and I thought at least we could be on friendly terms—I certainly wanted that. I let hope rise again. Again, it was destroyed. Two weeks after we had agreed that Lauren and I would move back, my lawyer called and told me Jason would not surrender the house. Instead, he had all the locks changed so I couldn't get in. There was no change of heart. I think I knew then that there never would be.

During this time, Jason was busy closing our joint banking account and putting extra locks on the house and light sensors. Four days after I left, he closed one joint account that had only five hundred dollars in it. I was shocked to think his mind could focus on this when he was losing his wife and daughter. He didn't care where we were staying or if we had money to live on; he did not know if we were safe, and he did not attempt to help us.

Still, for two months after our separation, Jason continued to say he wanted me to come back. I wanted to believe him and called him three times hoping to hear that he was sorry for the way he had treated me and that he intended—or at least would try—to change. Instead, the calls opened me up to more yelling, abuse, anger, and humiliation. I didn't know what to do with my own feelings. On the one hand, I wanted him to change and be the person I once thought he was. On the other hand, I was constantly in panic because the divorce was moving forward, and time was running out to save our marriage. Finally, Jason stopped trying to get me back. I'm convinced that his family urged him to let me go, and that's what he did.

After Jason's parents left, my foolish hope came back. I wanted to see him, to see if he had missed me. I went to the house on a Saturday on the pretense of checking for mail. I told a friend where I was going and asked her to watch out for me. I had my phone set to dial for emergency if anything frightening happened. Jason and I exchanged formal greetings and made small talk. All of a sudden, he asked me to have sex. I was dumbfounded. After the separation and all the bitterness, how could he even dream that I would want that at this time? His utter lack of sensitivity shocked me.

Jason began to phone and text again. As instructed by my lawyer, I didn't respond to him. The messages ranged from begging me to come back to cursing me for my disloyalty. I got used to this and took it in stride, but then after a month, things changed. I found out that Jason was telling stories about me at his work and at mine, the same lies that his parents were spreading. He would say that I was a bad person and out to get him. He tried to convince his coworkers and mine that I had physically hurt him and that I had stolen money, jewelry, and furniture from the house. He put me in the wrong by saying that I never gave him any idea that I intended to leave him, and he claimed that he would do anything to get Lauren and me back. He slandered me and tried to ruin my reputation. He did more than just talk; he sent e-mails to people who had been our friends and made all kinds of mean and untrue accusations.

One day at work, my supervisor called me into his office. Jason had contacted him indirectly through his manager with his foul stories about me. I had to defend myself against Jason's accusations. Jason had convinced himself that I would have my staff look up payroll data on him. But any data my staff could access had already been made available in the divorce proceedings; Jason was paranoid. At the end of the conversation, all was well between my supervisor and me, but I'll never get over the humiliation I felt at what Jason had done to me. He tried to make me lose my job and cripple me financially. He must have thought if that happened I would give up fighting for my daughter. How wrong he was about that.

I still marvel that I was able to continue to work and care for Lauren through all of this. It was all so strange—almost surreal. The lawyers, the judges, and the courts all frightened me and made me more anxious than ever. My mother stayed with me as long as she could, but after a few months she returned to Lebanon. Still, my parents kept in constant contact with me during all this time; I talked with them almost daily. They encouraged me, supported me, and sent money to help us. Without them, I don't think I would have been able to go through my divorce and come out in one piece.

AFTERMATH

Court dates, lawyers meetings, and lots of stress and anxiety threw a new curveball at me every day. Old friends never contacted me, and new friends I had made stabbed me in the back. The daycare owner who had helped Lauren and me shared with Jason all our conversations and activities during the month we had stayed with her; She was another betrayal waiting to happen. She even was audacious enough to tell me that Jason was buying her and the teachers gift cards from Macys; Since when he spent money on anyone? That wasn't free from his end, it came with a motive of turning her against me and buying her stories when I confided in her at my weakest. He even offered the principle of a private school that Lauren was attending prescription drugs to manipulate her; she refused and told me about it instead; he got us kicked out from that school by harassing the teachers and Lauren as it was told to my lawyer and his as well. Only one local Lebanese family cared and many pre-marriage friends who extended their helping hands. They believed me and believed in me. They helped me get more of my belongings from the house. Jason made me split all of our household goods in half, even my diet food and the baby wipes. I only took a few dishes and Lauren's bedroom furniture that I had bought for her. Jason kept everything else: every single piece of furniture and all the house goods. He even videotaped me collecting my belongings; nothing escaped his eyes or supervision.

My parents bought me new furniture for my newly rented apartment, and my sister gave me money for the deposit and the first month's rent until I got back on my feet. I found a second job that paid well, and I made a promise to my daughter that I would fight until my last breath and my last ounce of energy to keep her with me.

Every day since I left Jason has been a challenge: new dilemmas, tough choices, disturbing decisions, and unfavorable court rulings. As a loyal citizen, I abided by the law and shared visitations with Jason, as hard as it is for a mother to have to go several days without seeing her baby girl. During our marriage, he repeatedly told me that the best way to hurt a mother is by taking her daughter away. He kept trying to do just that. He desperately tried to prove me an unfit mother. He requested a psychological evaluation for me and used my anxiety as a reason for distrusting my sanity.

Jason will not be able to carry out that plan. I will defend my daughter to my last breath. I have never felt more mentally strong and emotionally stable. I have started working on a PhD degree to channel my negative energy into intellectual and academic activities. It has been hard to focus on my studies while I work at two jobs and tend to the divorce process, but Lauren has given me more strength than I knew I had. She has me now, but if I lose me, she loses me. I will not let that happen.

One day when I was bringing Lauren for her time with Jason, he got angry with me and slammed the car door on my hand, which caused minor bruising. Luckily, a witness called the police, and for the first time in our marital history, Jason was arrested and had to spend the night in jail. After all I have gone through in our marriage, I find it ironic that he was charged with domestic violence for the first time. He domestically violated me countless times. When I pressed charges, the state's attorney asked me what I wanted out of the court case. I said, "I want Jason to realize that abusing women is not a joke nor is it to be tolerated. I want Jason to be found guilty as charged. I don't ever want to see my daughter, his future wife, or any other woman having to give testimony against him or any other man for violence charges."

Him and I were ordered a no contact order. Few months later the state attorney's office decided to drop the charges where I was informed same day which violate the Illinois victim's right. The ruling was "Nolle Prosequi" which mean "no prosecution". The case didn't go to trial, the witness wasn't interviewed; his criminal lawyer knew for sure his was around the court. He later filed a motion for expungement to remove the arrest and jail time from his record and he won again. See Exhibit A. those records are no longer online after the expungement was granted; His justification to the judge was that he was applying for the US citizenship and it will affect his application. I didn't know the court of law was in the charity business; I couldn't get away with a traffic ticket.

Although I thought I left Jason purely for his inconsistent behavior; his narcissistic personality; his manipulations and mind games; his mental, physical, and emotional abuse, I was in for the surprise of my life when I learned of the ways he had cheated me financially. My lawyer called me and asked me a simple question: "Where were you the last two years of your marriage? How could you have not known about Jason's financial dealings that would hurt you and Lauren?" I was startled. She then informed me that for the past two years Jason had been wiring all of his money to his family in Canada, and she was dumbfounded that I didn't know about the transfer of funds. He had also signed over to them the investment house we had purchased in Arizona. He had created fake loans with his father to justify sending money out of the country, opened several new checking accounts, and made his father the beneficiary on his life insurance policy. Slowly, Jason had been taking away all the assets that belonged to us jointly in such a way that I would not be able to claim them in a divorce. He took from Lauren and me assets that were ours.

At first, all this information frightened me. I wasn't sure what to think; it all felt surreal. Had I no sense of reality? Was he creating so much drama that it turned my attention away from his wrongdoing? Jason had accused me for years of being delusional and crazy and in need of psychiatric help because I doubted him. Now I found I had much more reason to doubt than I ever knew. Then I realized his parents had been aware of how he had been transferring and hiding money all along and played me like an idiot while they kept telling me they loved me. They were accomplices to the scam. I felt the world was turning, and I got very sick.

It was a while before I could think straight again, but when I could, I realized that the truth the lawyer told me could set me free. I could look at events from a more realistic perspective. I discovered that while Jason was telling me he wanted me back, he was busy with financial arrangements that could only harm Lauren and me. While he was supposedly sad and traumatized in the first week after I left the house, he sold all our stocks, and he closed our savings account that had just five hundred dollars in it. To be sure no ready money was available, he paid off the mortgages on our home and on the house we purchased in Arizona. He even maintained he had financial interest in my jewelry and took back the jewelry his family had given me at the wedding along with several gold pieces Jason gave me since we married.

Since I filed for divorce Jason has been working full time on my character defamation around our work place and in the community. He tried manipulating doctors, and nurses even by taking nurses one on one in the echography room venting his victimized self. He didn't think of his self-respect nor of anyone else's specially me, the mother of his daughter. He had the public gossiping about false statements like him filing for divorce and leaving me because I was sleeping around in the marriage. I kept my head held high and prayed to God to vindicate me from this demonic burden. I never once uttered a word in retrospect, he was and always will be the father of my daughter and I never once allowed myself to slander him even in the face of all these accusations. People have all the right to believe his stories since most of them don't see through his manipulative and narcissistic personality and since they only heard his side and never mine; while Jason was busy covering the news in southern Illinois and maybe worldwide, I was busy raising my wonderful Lauren and spending with her every free minute making her a better person and on the path of faith and making sure she is not the child he always was.

After all that I've said here, I have to admit that the feeling of love I had for Jason has not yet left me. I remember the soft, sweet words he would occasionally speak to me and the times of romance. I miss his stopping by my office in the morning when he got off the night shift. That was always a special time. What is shocking is that I miss him every day and am even tempted to call him occasionally. After months of separation, my heart has forgotten the bad, and I am at peace with myself. I wonder if I should go back to him. Is there any chance that I can change him now? Then, I remember that no matter how much I loved him and cared for him, he could not change in the way that was needed to keep Lauren and me with him. And I need to remind myself of all that happened during our four years of marriage. Jason would abuse me in one way or another, I would forgive him, and we were both supposed to forget it and move on. I fell for his manipulation for years. Sometimes I feel I am still falling for it. Now, though, I can and do make the choice to resist manipulation. I must and will fight to keep myself and my precious child free of that way of life. Our divorce is still underway; it is a large and complicated divorce case as well as a criminal case against Jason. I pray that God keeps my daughter and me in safety and free from my husband's abuse and his family's manipulation and hypocrisy. I wish for them to find peace and stop attempting to turn my daughter against my family and me. Every time she visits with her dad, he takes time to teach her to hate, to resent, and to be negative. When she returns from these visits, she is quiet and introverted—totally unlike herself. I hope they truly know one day the meaning of love and compassion; they are missing out.

Over Christmas, my favorite holy season, I missed us as a family and decided to forgive and ask from him to attempt with me marriage counseling; my friends and family disapproved and I know why they would but they supported me never the less. I was receiving during those months insurance claims about him seeing a psychiatrist and innocent me I thought he is trying to change for me and I should reach out. My attempt was a failure because he refused marriage counseling; and I later found out that those psychotherapy sessions were his tool to getting out of the criminal case by saying he worked on his anger issues; well now it all make sense.

It was Lauren who gave me the greatest courage. In her love and trust for me, I saw just how important it was for me to continue to fight. We were together constantly when I wasn't working. We played, laughed, and cuddled—always close, always loving. You could say she became my soul mate. No matter how tired or busy I was, I made sure she was safe and had what she needed. I tried to protect her from anything that might hurt her. My every ambition for the future is tied up with Lauren. More than anything, I want her to be surrounded by love and to never have to face the trials I have faced in my four years of marriage. Lauren is my hope.

Jason played me like a doll during our marriage, and he made me suffer and beg every day of my life with him. Four years of Jason's torture was four years too many, and I'll never know how I endured it all that time. I am sure without him I will be just fine. I have found my strength, and I've found myself again. Jason was not successful in taking that away completely. I always wished he had truly loved me like a true man, not a coward manipulated by his delusions, paranoia, and hypocritical family. I am deeply grateful that I survived those four years and can move on.

DEDICATION TO JASON'S FAMILY

Luke 11:37–54

قال السيد المسيح «الويل لكم يا معلمي الشريعة... تغلقون ملكوت السماوات في وجوه الناس، فلا أنتم تدخلون، ولا تتركون الداخلين يدخلون... تأكلون بيوت الأرامل وأنتم تظهرون أنكم تطيلون الصلاة... تقطعون البحر والبر لتكسبوا واحداً إلى ديانتكم، فإذا نجحتم، جعلتموه يستحق جهنم ضعف ما أنتم تستحقون!... تعطون العُشر من النعنع والصعتر والكمون، ولكنكم تهملون أهم ما في الشريعة: العدل والرحمة والصدق... تصفون الماء من البعوضة، ولكنكم تبتلعون الجمل... تطهرون ظاهر الكأس والصحن، وباطنهما ممتلئ بما حصلتم عليه بالنهب والطمع... أنتم كالقبور المبيضة، ظاهرها جميل وباطنها ممتلئ بعظام الموتى وبكل فساد. وأنتم كذلك، تظهرون للناس صالحين وباطنكم كله رياء وشر.»

99

Exhibit A

***Jason's criminal charges before they were dropped and before the record
was removed***

Williamson County, IL | Case Dispositions

Williamson County, IL

NOTICE: By clicking the 'Search' button below, or otherwise using the Judici.com website

Last Search | Information | Dispositions | History | Payments | Fines & Fees

Name	No	Qualifier	Desc		Type	Date	Plea	Status
Count	1		Ticket Number: 267			05/06/2015		
Charge	1	Committed	DOMESTIC BATTERY/BODILY HARM		Original			Class A Misdemeanor

EXHIBIT B

Jason's insults; playing the victim almost every day; using God and gas-lighting to control me

Email from Jason

FYI, I didn't say my opinion yesterday about ur ugly dress yesterday... All without exception were clothed elegantly except you! Even Razan who isn't usually beautiful was like doll in her dress! Yours was the worst choice to the occasion.. With terribly opened dress showing all your back..
Obviously not helping to cover your breasts and width.. Making you a barrel shaped, ugly male looking as if trying to seduce with this unfitting opened back to the occasion!!
I loved the curly hair but your hair today and now is better than yesterday... Your style was squaring your rectangular face.. as if putting water on mud... With your short neck you looked like the stupid students in TV movies... I have told you many times not to square your face and you never listened.. The long hair does not fit all dress styles. ESP if closed from front, with your curved elderly back; called buffalo hump..
I saved you my opinion yesterday to give you some confidence... See the pictures and compare with what I said. I am not lying or exaggerating...

Email from Jason

Not only depression, not only anxiety.. You have total disturbances in your brain chemicals! I'm not judging but this is what I see!
The serotonin is messed up, u r more responsive to ZOFRAN (5HT3 serotonin blocker) rather than primperin.. At the same time you need serotonin stimulation by SSRI!

Obviously, you need treatment but doesn't work without behavioral reinforcement.. You need to act what is right regardless if you like it or not!
This is how civilized communities grow..
You need to abide by the speeding limit regardless of your emotions, act as a lady regardless.. truly I feel you act fiercely like a guy! Ladies are soft and smooth..
STOP SCREAMING IN MY FACE!!
Let Jesus live in your heart and pray hard for me.. I lost my patience accommodating you.. I can't tolerate more! I need prayers..

Email from Jason

YOU ARE SO POOR. Your taste in things is odd and happy about those few odd that like your taste!?? You are way uglier than the money you pay for anything! You think that expensive will make people think that you are beautiful, or showing your breasts with buttons opened make people not seeing your defects!!
I've never seen a beautiful girl with Karsh! Your tommy above your pant is so disgusting, drivers are ashamed of it.. All who I know in this area are well dressed on slim bodies.. You buy expensive from my sweat then expect to look beautiful.. You look exactly as you look with beautiful clothes that don't match your body, don't fit your feet nor harmonized with your personality!! All is messed up! If you don't see what shall I say.. Even Hala █████ has no tommy that you have after all these children!

101

Email from Jason (the hidden name is my daughter's name)

btw I reall appreciate what you are doing with ▆▆▆▆ she is doing fine with good health coz you are taking care of her well
You are clean. and feeding her well. I know that she should be kissing your feet when she is older!
You are a wonderful sacrifice and a model and I am grateful to have you as a wife
I love you much hobbi

Email from Jason

Listen, you HAVE TO UNDERSTAND THAT THERE IS ONE HEAD IN THIS HOUSE! If you want to be the head and take the decisions who have married the wrong wrong guy.
U should have married less smart guy, whom you can drive... Obviously you underestimate my capabilities since I come to you in a humble way to ask your advise and guess what, you hint even said that I am idiot!! Idiot is who doesn't take advise, but more stupid is the one who takes the advise from the wrong person... A man who was able to finish nephrology straight from the high school, without skipping any year, with no breaks is a very hard worker and obviously very intelligent... A man who can challenge your majors in environmental sciences, physics and Chemistry is obviously a smart one... I have managed my things by myself alone most of the time. I have never slept with a girl to help myself through a problem, I have never begged from anyone for help... But I was going straight in front of my Lord and God... He was my refuge and my castle, my salvation in my difficulties... He was the one who made my high mountains green meadows and was the cool water for my thirst.
He is still blessing me because of the prayers of my parents, because of His great mercy.
Obviously, I am going astray... But I am noticing my sins and they are in front of me always... I am dying spiritually as a cut branch, drying without the trunk... Jesus is the vine and we are the branches... Let's go to Jesus together.

Now again, two things you should know
I love you much, and don't take this phrase easy since it is true. I am myself deprived from hearing it and I wish hearing it from you..
I am sorry for all what upset you... I will work to satisfy you from my heart.

Email from Jason – He threatened to cheat on me and divorce me all along

BE CAREFUL. YOUR HUSBAND WILL SEEK AFFIRMATION SOMEWHERE

Have you ever noticed how the adulterous woman in the book of Proverbs seduces the unwitting young man? It's not with sex (okay, it's not just with sex), it's with flattery "She threw her arms around him... and with a brazen look she said, "I've offered my sacrifices and just finished my vows. It's you I was looking for!"... With her flattery she enticed him. He followed her at once" (from Proverbs 7)

Email from Jason

Oops, thank u for shouting back... So u claim that I raped u? Or the only thing that I didn't do? Wowwww
If u go to this low type of speech, it simply reflects your low class, imbalanced and permit me to say, your retarded thinking... U have obviously abnormal thinking processes and mood instability... U r mentally hazardous...
U attack the wrong per song in the wrong way.
Think again... I am ARABIC SON OF ARABIC NOT INDIAN BEGGER

Email from Jason

You don't have anything on me. I will decide and do my plans and inform you later as you do!!! Till now, I've not bought anything above 100$ without consulting you before... I feel idiot!

Email from Jason (the hidden name is my sister's name)

Notice how you made the problem and became crazy for nothing and wasted lots of energy even without me arguing with you.. you deprived me the good sleep because of your doubts.. and then you send ▆▆▆ that I am FULL OF DOUBTS... hehehe sure!
You have multiple psychiatric issues like OCD, anxiety, panic attacks and multiple phobias not me.. I see them and I have to deal with them quietly coz I love you. You are my perfect wife and the lady of my heart. I know we are humans and I AM full of sins.
Good day.

Email from Jason – as if all my doubts weren't proven correct after I filed for divorce

I don't know what is going on in your brain? But you are delusional these days: claiming that I do things or hide things or planning for things that are not true or right!! ▆▆▆ this is true disease! This is real and um not kidding! This is part of psychosis!
▆▆▆ you are claiming horrible things, saying bad stuff... Control your tongue and think before you say! THINK!! Don't be hasty!

Anyway, you need to treat your delusions, check with psychiatrist!! Dr ▆▆▆ is good one who comes to hospital... I think at Hermn! But please deal with facts, with reality not with your claims and your expectations!!!

Email from Jason

IM TRYING TO WEAR THE GARBAG STUFF THAT YOU BUY ME AND NOT WASTE IT. It does not work with anything . I hate everything you but. I hate your style and don't like it on me. You are poor.

Email from Jason

Hey, don't mix between an opinion and a fact, between past and present. I've not said that u r not attractive at any time within the last year, In between us you were at that point to me, and used it to hurt you while I'm angry trying to revenge for what you say daily. I've not said it recently and I bet you can

Email from Jason

Thank you for cooking but if you want to cook for me, cook what I like..
OIL IS DISGUSTING FOR ME AND YOU POUR TONS!!!!!
I HATE POTATO SANDWICHES, don't you know that!! Bread in bread is better!!!
I always oblige myself to eat what you cook though I don't like!! This one is disgusting. I couldn't even try the sandwich, I was going to vomit just thinking I have to eat it!
It's grace of God and I will oblige myself to eat it!

Email from Jason

I DON'T DOCUMENT AND STOP HALLUCINATING. Be Logic NOBODY NEEDS TO SEE THIS BS.
IF YOU THINK IT MAY BE USED FOR LEGAL ISSUES... BE COOL AND THERE WILL NEVER BE A LAWYER IN BETWEEN US, UNLESS WE ARE BOTH TRULY INSANELY CRAZY OR STUPIDIOTICS!!!

BE NORMAL AND LIVE NORMAL. GOD IS DOCUMENTING EVERYTHING AND IS A WITNESS ABOUT THE SACRFICE AND THE MISERY I PASS THROUGH DAILY.

Text from Jason

STOP TEXTING YOU LIAR..
You proved you malice and as a liar since the very beginning..

All the above is to say the least. A snapshot of my daily life. Jason never seized to play the victim and blamed the world for all his problems. He created realities and believed them and I had to find my sanity in the midst of it all.

www.ingramcontent.com/pod-product-compliance
Lightning Source LLC
Chambersburg PA
CBHW030957090426
42737CB00007B/568